Up with Hope

A Biography of

Jesse Jackson

BY DOROTHY CHAPLIK

A People in Focus Book

ꝺP | Dillon Press, Inc.
Minneapolis, Minnesota 55415

Photo Acknowledgments

AP/Wide World Photos—38, 85 (top), 89 (top), 90; The Chicago Defender—37, 40; Michael S. Green/The Detroit News—front cover, 8, 88, 89 (bottom); Otis Harrison/North Carolina Agricultural and Technical State University—34, 35; Jacques M. Chenet/Newsweek—back cover; Operation PUSH—39, 41, 84, 85 (bottom); Religious News Service—83; Rhoden Photo and Press Service—36; UPI/Bettman Newsphoto—86 (top), 87; The White House/Bill Fitz-Patrick—86 (bottom)

Library of Congress Cataloging in Publication Data

Chaplik, Dorothy.
  Up with hope.

  (People in focus)
  Bibliography: p.
  Includes index.
  Summary: Follows the life of the influential civil rights leader, covering his childhood, education, and work in the civil rights movement.
    1. Jackson, Jesse, 1941-   —Juvenile literature. 2. Afro-Americans—Biography—Juvenile literature. 3. Civil rights workers—United   States—Biography—Juvenile   literature. 4. Afro-Americans—Civil rights—Juvenile literature. [1. Jackson, Jesse, 1941-   . 2. Civil rights workers. 3. Afro-Americans—Biography] I. Title. II. Series.
E185.97.J25C43 1986   323.4'092'4 [B] [92]   86-11634
ISBN 0-87518-347-6

Dillon Press, Inc., 242 Portland Avenue South
Minneapolis, Minnesota 55415

Printed in the United States of America
  2 3 4 5 6 7 8 9 10 95 94 93 92 91 90 89 88 87

Contents

Text Acknowledgments

Pages 29 and 59: From Barbara A. Reynolds, *Jesse Jackson: America's David,* © 1985, JFJ Associates.

Page 95: From Joe Klein, "Travels with Jesse," © *People Weekly*, April 23, 1984.

Page 98: From D. Michael Cheers, "Campaigning for Jackson Is a Family Affair," reprinted by permission of *JET* Magazine, © 1984 Johnson Publishing Company, Inc.

Page 107: From "Interview with the Rev. Jesse Jackson," reprinted by permission of *Ebony* Magazine, © 1981 Johnson Publishing Company, Inc.

Acknowledgments

Without the help of the Reverend Jesse Jackson and many of his friends and relatives, this book would not have been the same. I am grateful to those people who talked with me about their early memories of Jesse Jackson, as well as their recent experiences. The generous giving of their time and thoughts went into the making of this biography.

From Greenville, South Carolina, there were conversations with Julius Kilgore, the Reverend J. D. Mathis, Horace Nash, Noah Robinson, Sr., and the Honorable Sara Shelton. In Chicago, I spoke to the Reverend Clay Evans, the Reverend Alvin Pitcher, Noah Robinson, Jr., and the Reverend Frank Watkins, as well as to the Reverend Jesse Jackson and Mrs. Jacqueline Jackson. Santita Jackson talked with me by telephone from Washington, D.C., and Dr. Howard Schomer spoke to me from Upper Montclair, New Jersey.

A special debt of gratitude goes to Barbara A. Reynolds, author of *Jesse Jackson: America's David*. The thorough research represented in her book provided valuable background material.

For reading the manuscript, I am indebted to my junior readers, Heather Narissa Culton and Ritu Dhaliwal, as well as to Muriel Levin and Birdell Provus. Thanks are also due my husband, Seymour Chaplik, whose help in every way was above and beyond the call of duty.

— Dorothy Chaplik

Introduction

". . .The most famous black man in America."

On a warm summer evening in 1984, millions of Americans watched their television sets as a handsome black man talked about his country. The rise and fall of his voice and the force of his words brought tears to many eyes.

The Reverend Jesse Louis Jackson was addressing the Democratic National Convention in San Francisco, California, on July 17, 1984. He was the first major black candidate to seek nomination for the presidency of the United States. He asked convention delegates to vote for him on their first ballot, but he agreed to support whoever they nominated.

Since his college days, Jesse Jackson had been active in the civil rights movement. As a student in Greensboro, North Carolina, he organized sit-ins and marches to protest segregation. Later he went to Chicago to study for the ministry. At that time he became an aide to Dr. Martin Luther King, Jr., head of the Southern Christian Leadership Conference (SCLC), a civil rights organization.

In Chicago, Dr. King appointed Jackson head of Operation Breadbasket, a branch of the SCLC. As its director, he helped create thousands of jobs for black workers. Later he founded Operation PUSH (People United to Serve Humanity) to improve living standards for blacks. His PUSH for Excellence project improved education goals in many schools in the country.

Reporters follow Jesse Jackson across the nation and around the world. In Europe, Africa, the Middle East, and Latin America, he has met with heads of state. Traveling to Syria, he won freedom for an American airman held captive there. On the fortieth anniversary of the end of World War II, he went to France to speak to the European Parliament. Recently, he became a leader in the fight against apartheid in South Africa.

At home and abroad, the Reverend Jesse Jackson is known for his gifted speech and his concern for those who suffer. Though he is often criticized, his harshest critics admit he is a brilliant speaker with a magnetic personality. Many people consider him the most famous black man in America today. His rise from humble beginnings is a remarkable story.

Up with Hope

Chapter/One

"Promise me you'll be somebody."

Even as a young boy, Jesse Louis Jackson had a reputation as a good talker. The people in his hometown do not remember him as a fighter, though he was always bigger than most kids his age. Where other boys used their fists, Jesse was expert with words. On the playground he was usually surrounded by children—Jesse talking, the others listening. In the classroom he spoke out easily, when most kids were shy and fumbling for the right words.

Jesse began speaking in public when he was very young. By age four, he was acting in church plays. His good memory and his ease in front of an audience made him a star. At nine, he represented his Sunday school at a convention in another city, and he made an oral report every month to the full congregation. In high school, Jesse's talent with words and his quick wit made him the school comedian. He liked to tell jokes and funny stories. His classmates were sure he was going to be a professional entertainer.

His gift with words came from both sides of the family.

On his natural father's side, there were several Baptist preachers. Lively language was second nature to them. On the other side of the family, his mother and grandmother loved words. His mother expressed herself in song. She sang spirituals in church and performed in operettas at school. His grandmother was a woman of ready speech. As Jesse grew up, she filled his ears with familiar southern phrases that gave him love and inspiration to last a lifetime.

While he was growing up, Jesse was ashamed of his life's beginnings. Today, the Reverend Jesse Jackson often tells the story of his birth from the stage of his church in Chicago.

In 1941, Greenville, South Carolina, was a quiet, proper town. Churchgoing black people were shocked when they heard that Helen Burns was expecting a baby. Helen Burns was not married. The baby's father, Noah Louis Robinson, lived next door and had another family.

Many people in Greenville urged Helen Burns to marry someone before the child was born. But she cared very much for Noah Robinson and refused to marry anyone else. As a result, she was not allowed to attend the Springfield Baptist Church, although she had been a lifelong member. Helen held her head high as she went about her daily life and tried to ignore the gossip around her.

Noah Robinson, a textile worker, openly admitted he was the father of the expected baby. An amateur boxing champion, Robinson was not a man people dared to offend. Most people did not tell him so directly, but they disapproved of his fathering a child outside of marriage.

(Later, when young Jesse was old enough to be on the playground, he, too, felt the community's disapproval. He has never forgotten the first time a group of boys made fun of him. They called out that he was a nothing and a nobody because he had no daddy. Jesse hid his pain and vowed that one day he would prove he was somebody.)

For all the community's objections, Jesse Louis was born on October 8, 1941, in the white cottage on Haynie Street where his mother lived. Helen Burns was eighteen years old at the time. She had dropped out of high school after her junior year to have her baby.

Handsome Noah Robinson was fond of Helen Burns and proud of his young son. He and Helen talked with Helen's mother, Matilda Burns, about what to call the infant. They agreed to name him after Noah's father, the Reverend Jesse Robinson. The Reverend Jesse Robinson and his twin brother, Jacob, also a minister, had founded the Mount Emmanuel Baptist Church in Greenville. Their three brothers were preachers, too, and all were descendants of the Cherokee Indians. Ella Robinson, Noah's mother, had been a slave and the daughter of an Irish plantation owner. The Reverend Jesse Robinson and Ella Robinson died before young Jesse's birth, so Jesse never knew them.

Noah Robinson helped provide for his son and visited him often as he grew up. But as time went by, he was less involved in the little boy's life.

When Jesse was two, his mother married twenty-four-year-old Charles Henry Jackson. To take care of his new family, Jackson gave up his dream of playing professional baseball and took a job at the post office. Soon they moved to a different neighborhood on the other side of town. Though their house was run-down and shabby, they lived better than many black families in town. Before long, Jesse was calling his new father Daddy.

Jesse's stepfather was good to him, but Jesse missed being a part of his natural father's family. Well mannered and well dressed, Noah Robinson was a church deacon and was respected in the community. The oldest of his three sons was Noah, Junior, who was close to Jesse in age. When Noah, Junior, was five or six, he learned that Jesse was his brother. He never forgot that day.

Noah, Junior, says, "I was playing in front of our house and saw a little boy across the street, standing on the edge of the playground. He was staring at our house and I was staring at him. It was strange because we looked so much alike. We were almost the same size and height and had the same curly hair. Most of the people in my family and in our neighborhood had straight hair."

Noah, Junior, was curious and ran to get his father, who sat down and explained that he had another brother. Later he brought Jesse to the house and introduced him.

In the years that followed, Jesse often stood in front of the Robinson's home, staring into their windows. His father did not always see him—sometimes Noah, Junior, had to let him know Jesse was there. As soon as his father waved from the window, Jesse would wave back and run away.

Jackson still remembers how big and beautiful his father's house looked to him then. It was surrounded by green grass and flowers. His own home, small and humble, was crowded against other houses just like it. In their scratchy dirt yard, his family raised chickens.

When Jesse was growing up in the 1940s, Greenville had a population of 62,000. Located in the foothills of the Blue Ridge Mountains, it was the textile capital of the world. Fifteen percent of the population was black, and most of the black people worked in textile mills or shirt factories or private homes.

The black community where Jesse lived had the closeness of a large family. People knew nothing of the violence and fear of one another that strangers in a large city often live with today. Before going off to work in the morning, adults drank coffee together on their front porches. If there was sickness or death in a family, everyone in the community helped.

At that time, the civil rights movement had not yet begun in the South. The same laws existed that were practiced in the days of slavery. The laws gave all authority to white people and denied basic rights to blacks, who were not even allowed to vote. The laws prevented black people and white people from living in the same section of town and attending the same churches and schools. Blacks and whites ate in separate restaurants, used separate restrooms, and drank from separate water fountains.

Jesse Jackson remembers the "Whites Only" signs around town and how kids would lie to themselves to keep from feeling hurt. He says, "We would say we didn't want to drink water because we weren't thirsty, or we didn't want to eat because we weren't hungry, or we didn't want to go to the movie theater because we didn't want to see the picture."

Antiblack attitudes were not as bad in Greenville as in other southern towns. Racism existed there, but it existed peacefully. The same year that Jesse was born, the Ku Klux Klan (KKK) made its last march through Greenville. Other towns continued to fear its attacks.

The KKK marchers usually came into town at night, wearing long white robes and masks. They carried burning crosses and threatened violence. All-white police forces often ignored them, in spite of the violence and deaths they caused. The KKK worked to keep white supremacy, to keep all the power in the hands of white people.

The meaning of white supremacy became clear to Jesse because of two things that happened in his childhood. When he was five or six, he entered a neighborhood store where he and his friends often bought candy and cookies. The grocer was waiting on other customers. Jesse was in a hurry and said, "Jack, I need some candy right away." He whistled to catch the grocer's attention. Suddenly Jack wheeled around, reached under the counter for a gun, and pointed it at Jesse's face. "Don't ever whistle at a white man again as long as you live," he said. Although the store was filled with people, no one came forward to help Jesse. He was trembling as he left the store, and he sensed that every black person there shared his fear.

Another time, Jesse was excited by a boxing match between a black champion, Joe Louis, and a white man. He explains: "A group of us kids was gathered in front of a cigar store listening to the radio. Joe Louis was battering the white guy without mercy. But we didn't dare show any emotion over a black man beating a white one. We knew it would anger the white shopkeeper and his friends." After listening silently, Jesse ran home, where he could safely let out a cheer for Louis.

The bitterness of living with white supremacy was partly offset by the warm, tender atmosphere of Jesse's home. He remembers his grandmother Matilda Burns as "a very loving and caring person." He says, "She made great sacrifices for my mother and me in our early years." Known as Aunt

Tibby, his grandmother was a source of strength to him.

Although she never learned to read or write, Aunt Tibby knew the importance of books and education. When Jesse was growing up, she earned money by working in the homes of white people in town. At one home she kept her eye on the books and magazines being read by the young son of her employer. When he was finished, Aunt Tibby brought them home. Magazines like *National Geographic* opened Jesse's view of the wide world outside of Greenville.

The day the first television set arrived in Jesse's neighborhood, people were excited. They crowded into the owner's house to see "The Lone Ranger." But there was a problem when it was time for the news. Instead of being announced, the news came across the screen in silent words. Of the sixty people in the room, Jesse was the only one who could read. At the time he felt important. Later he realized how sad it was that so many adults could not read.

Aunt Tibby taught Jesse other valuable lessons. "Avoid violence," she said, and, "Always be clean. Cleanliness is next to Godliness." She also taught him to use good manners and to respect other people, even those who did not respect him. This was not an easy lesson to learn in a town where white people showed little respect for blacks.

But not for a moment did Aunt Tibby allow her grandson to feel that he was less worthy than anyone else. She let him know she thought he was exceptional. "When God made you, he did his best work," she said. Other times she urged, "Jesse, promise me you'll be somebody."

Along with love and encouragement, Jesse was brought up with discipline and religion. His family's life-style was built around the Bible. Jackson says, "It was the most important book in the house. My earliest heroes were from the Bible—David, Joseph, Samson, Paul."

His mother and stepfather were devoted churchgoers. They worshipped twice on Sundays. The Jacksons and their two sons (Jesse and his younger brother, Charles) walked three miles to the Longbranch Baptist Church, where both parents sang in the choir. The soulful singing, the chanting and hand clapping, and the preacher's fiery speeches provided memories Jesse never forgot.

The Jacksons raised Jesse and Charles with the idea that work was as important as religion. They believed that work would keep the boys out of trouble when they were not in church or school.

Jesse's first job, at the age of six, was in the wood and coal yards owned by his grandfather. The two drove to the country in an old pickup truck and gathered pieces of lumber. After the wood was sawed into stove-length slabs, they delivered the slabs around the neighborhood for twenty or twenty-five cents a bucketful. When the wood was taken care of, Jesse worked on the coal truck. Other times he raked leaves, cut grass, and ran errands. By the time he was eleven and in the fourth grade, he was in charge of the wood yard. By then he was better educated than most of the twenty men working there. He hired and fired workers, collected the money, and made out the payroll.

Jesse had other jobs, too. At eight, he sold souvenirs and snacks at Greenville's football stadium. (Jesse had to talk his way into that job, because it had been reserved for white boys until then.) At ten, he shined shoes in his stepfather's shop. Later he collected tickets at the Liberty Theater. At twelve, he caddied at the Greenville Country Club.

The money he earned kept Jesse well dressed. Clothes were important to him and to his friends. When they were shining shoes or caddying, the boys admired the way white people dressed and imitated their style. It helped make up for the feeling that they weren't as good as white people.

Almost daily Jesse struggled with the idea that he was not as good as other people. It was difficult growing up in the South at a time when white people did not accept blacks as equals. Not belonging to his natural father's family also brought him pain and anger. The hurt was made worse by the community's disapproval of his birth.

Jesse's ease with words helped him express his anger. With friends at school, on the street, or at home with his family, the words came tumbling out. Making jokes, heaping insults, pretending he was better and smarter than others helped Jesse get rid of some of the anger. Discovering sports helped, too.

Chapter/Two

"He played every game to win."

In grade school Jesse was a good student, but sometimes he was full of mischief. Once in a while his sixth-grade teacher put him in his place with the slap of a ruler. At times she and his mother had to remind him that school was a place to study, not play. In those early days, he often showed more interest in sports than in school.

If Jesse did not behave, he had to face his preacher, as well as his teacher and his parents. The preacher might scold Jesse publicly in church. If his behavior was very bad, they all got together at his home. Looking back now, Jackson sees the interest of the home, the school, and the church as "a love triangle." It kept him and most youngsters on the right path. For Jesse, the triangle began his first day of school in 1947, when his mother came along to meet his teacher. The following Sunday, he and the other first graders were taken to church, where an announcement was made that they had begun school. That three-sided love and concern continued all through his school years.

Mrs. Sara Shelton, his sixth-grade teacher, can still picture Jesse at the age of twelve—big and awkward, towering over her. Even then he had a sparkling personality and talked about wanting to be a football star.

There was another side to twelve-year-old Jesse. When his class wanted to carry out experiments for science, he thought of a way to earn money for equipment. He volunteered his mother's services and their home for a Sunday afternoon fund-raising tea. Luckily, Mrs. Jackson cooperated, and the fund raiser was successful.

Mrs. Shelton recalls her sadness when she faced gifted young students like Jesse in those days, because there was little opportunity to develop their talents. She says, "There was nothing to look forward to for blacks." Just the same, teachers and preachers worked hard to teach young black people to be the best possible human beings.

Black children in Greenville attended all-black schools with double sessions. Some students went to morning classes, others attended in the afternoon. They read old textbooks that white students no longer used. When there were not enough books to go around, five or six students shared a single book. When there was homework, no one could take the book home.

By the time Jesse was in sixth grade, he was already a good reader and had joined the reading club at the County Library for the Colored. The library was in the community center and was no more than a small reading room. Books were furnished by the main library as well as by people in the neighborhood. Here Jesse found books to satisfy his curiosity and his love for words.

Most of Jesse's teachers observed his reading skill, just

as they noticed his need for attention. He held opinions on most subjects and was always eager to express them. He ran in every school election and wanted desperately to win each of them.

His friends enjoyed his quick mind and found him loyal and generous. When he worked as a ticket collector at the Liberty Theater, he let his friends in free. Noah, Junior, remembers coming to the theater with his brothers: "Jesse would tell us to go around to the back and he would open the back door and let us sneak in."

Though Jesse was popular, some students found his drive to succeed hard to handle. Others teased him because of the spotless, fancy clothes he wore. Jesse took the teasing good-naturedly.

Most of Jesse's clothes came from the Opportunity Shop in Greenville, where white people brought things they no longer needed. He searched the shelves for brand-name shoes and other good-looking items. Townspeople still remember how well dressed he always was.

Jesse's teachers understood his need to dress well. They saw that beneath his fierce desire to be Number One in everything, and beneath his great show of confidence, he was painfully unsure of himself.

As he entered high school in 1955, Jesse felt a growing ambition to amount to something. He needed to prove to himself and to everyone that he was really somebody.

The ambition to be somebody could have led him in another direction. Like other boys in the neighborhood, he showed up at corner hangouts and learned to play black-jack, pitty-pat, and dirty hearts. His street friends called him Bo, short for Bo-Diddley, and he shot pool and threw dice with them. His mother disapproved of gambling, and he never told her about it. Knowing his family's high hopes for him kept Jesse from getting too involved in street life. His strong conscience never allowed him to miss a day of school or a Sunday church service.

Good, honest jobs were hard to come by in those days. Jesse knew people who sold illegal liquor, baseball tickets, and whatever they could get their hands on to make money. He saw these things going on, but did not get involved. Some of the boys he knew in his youth became drug addicts, alcoholics, and convicts. Today he says, "If it were not for the grace of God, I'd still be on the corner."

But Jesse found good jobs. When he was a high school student, he waited tables at the Poinsett Hotel and cleaned machinery on weekends at Claussen's bakery. He and his friend Owen Perkins complained about the "Whites Only" restrooms and drinking fountains at the bakery. They tried to organize the employees to protest their working conditions, but they were not successful.

Jesse's attempt to protest segregation at the bakery was inspired by a young black preacher in Greenville. The Reverend James Hall was adviser to the youth chapter of the NAACP (National Association for the Advancement of Colored People). In 1955, he introduced the idea of social action to improve the lives of people in the black community. That was the first time fourteen-year-old Jesse had heard of social action, something he did not fully understand until later, when one of his sports heroes came to town.

Jackie Robinson, a major league baseball player, arrived in Greenville by plane. Officials at the airport refused to let him enter the restaurant there because he was black. Mr.

Hall organized a march to protest the discrimination. He urged the black population to speak out for their rights. This experience with social action made Jesse aware of his right to demand justice.

At the all-black Sterling High School in Greenville, Jesse's classmates recognized his leadership qualities. Not only did they elect him president of the freshman class, but they made him president of the honor society and of the student council.

Some students resented his ambition and success. Jesse's high school French teacher, Mrs. Xanthene Norris, remembers hearing complaints about his winning everything. Some kids said that other people ought to have a chance. Of course, there were always other candidates running for office, but Jesse usually won.

He was not satisfied with winning all the elections. He worked hard to be excellent in his studies, outstanding as an athlete, and popular with the girls. He pored over the dictionary to learn more words and to improve his already first-rate speaking ability.

Mrs. Norris says he was the only football player in her classes to ask for homework when he was going to be absent for football practice. The others made excuses, but Jesse wanted to keep up his grades.

Mrs. Norris and Jesse had long talks together. Usually he talked about himself and his achievements. It seemed to her that he needed constant success in order to prove to himself that he really was somebody.

Jesse's half brother Noah, Junior, was also a student of Mrs. Norris, and she remembers how different they were. At times she had to coax Noah to talk, while she often had to stop Jesse from talking too much. She thought Noah was more secure because he had both his natural parents. Both boys did well in school. Noah graduated third in his class, while Jesse graduated tenth.

Noah remembers how funny Jesse was in high school. He says, "All the big guys with letters would sit together at lunchtime. Jesse would be there holding court. He was like Richard Pryor, Bill Cosby and Redd Foxx combined. He had the whole place cracking up."

Jesse's success in sports helped him gain confidence in himself. His stepfather had been an athlete, and he worked with both of his sons to develop their skills. Many of the boys in the neighborhood came over to the Jackson's backyard to use their hoop for basketball practice.

Sterling High's athletic coach, the Reverend J. D. Mathis, worked with Jesse from age thirteen to age seventeen. He says, "Jesse was an excellent, all-around athlete. Over six feet tall and weighing about two hundred pounds, he was a fierce competitor. He played every game to win." During the high school years, Jesse came away with letters in baseball, basketball, and football.

On the football field, Coach Mathis rated Jesse as the finest quarterback he had ever coached. He says, "He was bigger and stronger than most of the linemen, and swift and clean in his play. An all-American type."

Coach Mathis encouraged all athletes at Sterling to develop their minds along with their bodies. But Jesse did not need to be told to study. By the time he got to high school, he was already an ambitious student.

Julius Kilgore, his English teacher at Sterling High, remembers Jesse's great desire to get ahead. It often made him impatient with students who came to class unprepared. One day a student who was reading aloud in front of the class kept mispronouncing words. After several minutes of this, Jesse lost his temper. He burst out, "You need to go home and study your lesson." It annoyed Jesse that the student was holding the class back.

While he was in high school, sports absorbed a lot of Jesse's energy. In spite of segregation and racism, the athletes themselves were fair about one another. When a white player handled the ball well, the black athletes admitted it.

Sometimes Jesse and his friends went to the all-white Greenville High and played against the white team. The police stopped the games when they found out they were taking place, since the law did not allow blacks and whites to play together. Still, the white players often showed up on Thursdays to watch the Sterling football games, and the black athletes came to the Greenville games on Fridays.

At first Jesse thought it was too bad he couldn't play on the white team. Later, when he believed his team was the better one, he thought it was too bad the white athletes couldn't play on the black team.

Greenville's newspaper did not cover black games and white games equally. Jackson remembers the night he scored three touchdowns. He made nineteen points, and his team beat the school it was playing, 20 to 6. The all-white school won its game with a score of 7 to 6. Greenville High's quarterback, Dickie Dietz, had kicked the extra point. Big headlines in the newspaper stated, "Dietz kicks extra point. Greenville wins." A small column at the bottom of the page read, "Jackson makes three touchdowns. Sterling wins." The unequal coverage was unfair, and it bothered Jesse.

In the summer of 1959, after graduating from high school, Jesse attended a professional baseball tryout camp. He was the only black athlete to come. Already he had a good reputation as a pitcher, averaging about seventeen strikeouts a game. However, the two Chicago White Sox scouts at the camp had come to see Dickie Dietz. Even in high school, Jackson says, Dietz could hit a ball a mile. The scouts asked Jesse to pitch for Dietz. He struck Dietz out three times and caught one foul tip. As a result of the tryout, Jesse was offered a job playing baseball for the White Sox.

The New York Giants topped the Chicago White Sox' offer. They were willing to pay Jesse six thousand dollars a year to join their team, plus a chance to go to school in the off-season. But the same club offered Dickie Dietz ninety-five thousand dollars. The difference in the amounts offered a white man and a black man brought the meaning of racism home to Jesse in a new way.

Instead of playing professional baseball, Jesse accepted an athletic scholarship offered by the University of Illinois. He dreamed of being the first black quarterback on a major football team in the North. Maybe then he truly would be somebody.

Chapter/Three

"The call to preach."

Jesse Jackson's dream to play quarterback on the University of Illinois team was quickly shattered. When he reported for football practice in the fall of 1959, the coach informed him that blacks never were allowed to play quarterback. No matter what their abilities were, they had to be linemen.

In general, Jesse met with frustration on campus. Segregation was as bad there as in the South, if not worse. On weekends, black students had no place to go. White students partied in their large fraternity and sorority houses. Black students, Jackson recalls, "sat in their dorm drinking Coke and playing cards."

Every fall the big event on campus was the interfraternity dance. Jesse had joined an all-black fraternity and looked forward to the evening. He was disappointed to find the university's three black fraternities were not invited. He and his friends ended up at the Veterans of Foreign Wars lodge, listening to records. The white students, he says, "were jumping to Lionel Hampton in the gym. Live."

At home in Greenville for the Christmas holidays, Jesse was angered once again by southern racism. Because he was black, he was not allowed to use the main Greenville library. In order to complete school assignments, he cut short his vacation by four days and returned to school.

But segregation in the North was no easier to bear. By the end of his freshman year, Jesse decided to transfer to another school. The racism in sports and in social situations was one reason for his decision. Another reason was that Jesse was homesick. He missed his family and his friends and the glow of popularity he had enjoyed at Sterling High.

An even stronger reason came from a television report he watched in February of 1960. The report showed four students from North Carolina Agricultural and Technical State College (A&T), a small, all-black school. The students took seats at the all-white lunch counter of a Woolworth store in downtown Greensboro and ordered coffee. When the staff refused to serve them, the students took out their books and began to study. They refused to move, and the police were called to carry them out. Once the press picked up the story, black students all over the South began to stage sit-ins.

The student protest in Greensboro was the beginning of the second phase of the civil rights movement. The first major phase occurred in Montgomery, Alabama, in 1955 and 1956. At that time the black population, led by Dr. Martin Luther King, Jr., boycotted (refused to ride) the city buses for about a year. It was their protest against racial segregation on public transportation. Dr. King urged blacks to "walk in dignity rather than ride in shame." Jesse understood too well how the Greensboro students felt. He remembered the lesson in social action he had learned as a fourteen year old from the Reverend James Hall.

At the semester's end, Jesse left the University of Illinois and enrolled at North Carolina A&T. He quickly became a part of the action.

The young man from Greenville, South Carolina, felt at home in Greensboro, North Carolina. Just as he had done at Sterling High, Jesse leaped into positions of leadership at A&T. He became president of the student body and an officer of the Omega Psi Phi fraternity. On the football team, he was star quarterback. None of these activities interfered with his studies or his social life. He continued to be an honor student and to be popular with the girls. And he became very involved in the civil rights movement.

On his arrival at A&T, Jesse complained that the sit-ins were not bringing about change fast enough. The sit-ins were run by the Congress of Racial Equality (CORE). The students in charge challenged him to do a better job. He accepted the challenge and succeeded in speeding things up.

Instead of demonstrating every few months, he led marches through downtown Greensboro almost daily. His method was to enter white stores, hotels, restaurants, and theaters alone. If service or tickets were refused, black students formed sit-ins, picket lines, or mass demonstrations. They ignored the jeering of white youths and the little kids running alongside them, chanting, "Two, four, six, eight, we don't want to integrate."

While the sit-ins and marches were going on, Jesse talked frequently with one of his professors, Dr. Leonard Robinson. They discussed the meaning of protest, and Dr. Robinson gave him books to read to develop his thinking.

Under Robinson's influence, Jesse became familiar with the ideas of black leaders such as William E. B. Du Bois, Frederick Douglass, Booker T. Washington, and Marcus Garvey.

Continuing his protests, Jesse was arrested in June of 1963 for inciting a riot in downtown Greensboro. He had led a column of students in a sit-down demonstration in the middle of a busy street in front of the municipal building. When he was arrested, Jesse refused to post bond. He packed an overnight kit and prepared to go to jail. It was for something he believed in deeply, and he said, "I'm going without fear. I'll go to jail and I'll go to the chain gang if necessary."

At the jail, four hundred black protesters were forced into space meant for two hundred people. It was hot and stuffy. Jesse cried as he saw blacks suffocating and passing out. He promised himself that he would fight such unfair treatment the rest of his life.

In spite of the arrests, Jesse's leadership brought integration to downtown Greensboro. To honor his achievement, the governor of North Carolina appointed him to the state's student council on human rights.

By this time, Jesse's personal life was also very full. In 1960, shortly after transferring to A&T, he had met a young woman also involved in the civil rights movement in Greensboro. Jacqueline Lavinia Davis was a tiny, attractive girl from Virginia. She was a freshman and Jesse was a sophomore.

After their first meeting, Jacqueline was not sure she was going to like Jesse. He stood with a group of football players outside the student hall on campus. As she walked by in new, black suede shoes with high heels, he shouted, "Hey, baby, I'm going to marry you!"

Jesse's remark threw Jacqueline off balance. She says, "I stepped into a mud puddle and ruined my shoes. That put us on bad terms to start with, although he said he was sorry and offered to help me. But when we met later in a class we had together, I found him to be very bright and sensitive."

Jesse was her first boyfriend, but she quickly saw he was an unusual person. To begin with, not many football players were honor students. When football practice was over, all the other guys would parade around the campus. But Jesse would stay in his room studying, because he wanted to make the honor roll.

Going to church every Sunday, as he did, was also unusual for a student. Although Jacqueline had been a churchgoer all her life, she took a break from it at college. Jesse, however, wanted her to attend church. When he began lecturing her about it, his gift with words won out. She says, "After a while, I gave in and I have been going to church ever since."

They were married in 1962, in the living room of Jesse's parents' home in Greenville. Jacqueline Jackson remembers it as "a lovely little country wedding." Her gown, which she had sewn herself, was creamy white with a long train. One of the Greenville neighbors owned a flower shop and sent over a tall arch hung with flowers. It stood in front of the fireplace and was the setting for the ceremony. Other neighbors brought blankets, cakes, and small gifts. Jacqueline's parents came from Virginia for the wedding. Her younger sisters and brothers stayed at home and listened to the ceremony on the telephone.

In June of 1963, as Jesse was being released from jail in Greensboro, Jacqueline gave birth to their daughter, Santita. Both events meant changes. Having a family brought new responsibilities and joy to the Jacksons' personal life. Their success in integrating Greensboro meant improved conditions were on the way for black people in the South.

Having a child did not keep Jacqueline Jackson from joining her husband in civil rights demonstrations. If she had no babysitter, she took her daughter along to the picket line. At this time the Jacksons lived with friends or with people who believed in their cause. Looking back to those days, Mrs. Jackson says, "It was a time in the South when people took you in. You stayed with everybody and you shared everything." Even the doctor who delivered their baby refused to charge them, knowing they were poor students.

In his senior year, Jesse was drawn more deeply into the civil rights movement. He followed closely the victory won in Birmingham, Alabama, in 1963. Led by Dr. Martin Luther King, Jr., black people demonstrated against the city's harsh segregation laws. Their peaceful protests were met with violence from the city's police. Hundreds of people were attacked and arrested. President John F. Kennedy sent a deputy to help end the crisis. After a month of violence, white leaders finally agreed to desegregate their stores and to drop charges against the demonstrators.

In 1964, a civil rights bill sent to Congress by President Kennedy was passed and signed into law by President Lyndon B. Johnson. Dr. King was invited to the White House to be present at the signing.

As a student leader, Jesse attended the nonviolence

workshops conducted by Dr. King. Jesse was one of many
students, and he knew the civil rights leader only from a
distance. However, his respect for Dr. King made him re-
think his plans for the future.

For a while Jesse had considered going to law school. He
had thought it might make him a strong leader of his people.
However, as he watched Dr. King, Malcolm X (a leader of
the Black Muslims), and other people of authority, he realized that many civil rights leaders were ministers. The
black community respected its ministers, and the ministers
influenced large numbers of people. He remembered there
were many preachers on his father's side of the family.

According to his father, Jesse had dreamed of becoming
a preacher when he was about fourteen years old. Mr.
Robinson says, "Jesse told me he dreamed he would lead an
army across the waters like Moses did." His father told him
that even if he did not lead an army, he could be a fine
preacher some day, just as his grandfather had been.

For a long time Jesse had felt a growing urge to preach,
but he wasn't sure he had received "the call" (he had always
expected a call to preach to come as it had to Saint Paul, who
encountered the Lord on the road to Damascus). Today he
says, "The call to preach was slow to develop in me. It was
part of wanting to change the conditions under which I was
living."

As he neared graduation, Jesse discussed his future with
the campus minister and with Dr. Samuel Proctor, the
president of his school. Both men encouraged him to get
more education. Dr. Proctor advised him to take the call to
preach seriously. He said that the call could come to Jesse as
a certain feeling that he had a mission to carry out.

Jesse struggled a long time before making a decision. After graduation he did political work in North Carolina. He spent several weeks with Noah, Junior, who was a college student while living in New Jersey. All that time Jesse brooded about his future. Should he continue his education or should he go to Atlanta and join Dr. King? Should he study the law or the Bible? In the end, he took Dr. Proctor's advice and decided to become a minister.

All his life Jesse had been a steady churchgoer, just as his parents had been. At college, he was superintendent of the campus Sunday school. He insisted that all his fraternity brothers—and Jacqueline—go to classes with him each Sunday.

Still, his decision to become a minister surprised some of his friends. They knew he respected the ministers he met in the civil rights movement. On the other hand, he was outspoken in his dislike for other southern black preachers. He disapproved of those who taught their congregations to look for rewards in the next world, after death. Jesse wanted people to be rewarded in this world, by having the injustices removed from their lives.

His decision finally made, Jesse Jackson arrived in Chicago in 1964 with his wife and small daughter. He had accepted a scholarship to study for the ministry at the Chicago Theological Seminary. Once the decision was made, he felt relieved. Life would be quiet and peaceful, he thought, while he attended graduate school.

JESSE JACKSON

A & T Honor Student Is Elected
To National Fraternity Post

An honor student and football star at A&T College has been elected second vice grand basileus 'he Omega Psi Phi fraternity.
 ~con C~   ''' C C

Indianapolis, Indiana.
Jackson was elected second vice district representative of the Omega Psi Phi Sixth Distri^'
 ^ w^~   'ly :

(Above) In school, and especially at North Carolina A&T, Jesse Jackson was an excellent student and athlete, yet found time to be a leader in both student government and social organizations.

(Left) Jackson became deeply involved in the struggle for civil rights while still in college. Inspired by the leadership of Dr. Martin Luther King, Jr., Jesse worked with other students to desegregate downtown Greensboro, North Carolina.

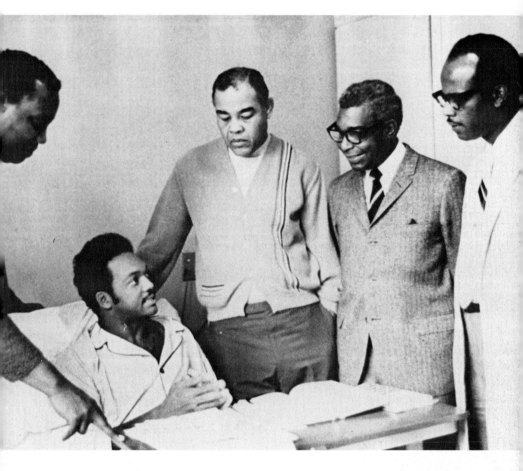

(Above) In 1968 doctors discovered that Jackson had sickle cell trait, a blood disease affecting mostly blacks of West African descent. Despite being hospitalized, Jesse kept working on such Operation Breadbasket events as Black Christmas and meeting with Breadbasket staff and friends, such as the Reverend G. Ed. Riddicks, Joe Louis (the former boxer), George Jones, and Jackson's personal physician, Dr. Andrew Thomas.

(Left) Jesse Jackson was at the Memphis, Tennessee, motel at the moment Dr. Martin Luther King, Jr. was assassinated. Jackson grieved deeply at King's funeral. Later, Jackson would become one of the leaders carrying on the fight for black equality.

Jesse Jackson did not quite finish his studies at the Chicago Theological Seminary because he began working full time for Operation Breadbasket; however, he was ordained a minister in 1968 and received an honorary degree from the Seminary in 1969. Here he is with two of his sons, Jesse, Junior and Jonathan Luther; his daughter Santita; and his wife Jacqueline.

In the SCLC's Black Expos, and later in PUSH Expos, businesses owned by blacks or serving blacks exhibited their goods and services. PUSH promoted black-owned businesses and pressured many white-owned businesses to hire more blacks.

In 1971 Jesse started his own organization, People United to Save (later, Serve) Humanity (PUSH). PUSH continued the fight for an end to discrimination, especially in housing and employment.

Jesse Jackson's family has given him love and inspiration throughout his life, and have themselves taken part in many of the events and activities in which Jesse has been involved. *(Top left)* Pictured are his mother, Helen Jackson; his stepfather, Charles Jackson; his grandmother, Matilda Burns (Aunt Tibby); his son Jonathan; and his daughter Santita. *(Below left)* Jesse Jackson with his half-brother Noah Robinson, Jr.; Noah and Jesse worked together briefly in Operation Breadbasket. *(Above)* The Jackson family in 1975; in front is Yusef; in the row behind him is Jonathan, the Reverend Jackson, and Jacky; in the back are Jesse, Junior, Santita, and Mrs. Jacqueline Jackson.

Chapter/Four

". . .Not afraid of violence and bullets and bombs."

Graduate school turned out to be much harder than college. Jesse had to do more reading, more writing, and more deep thinking as he studied to become a minister. His professors at the Chicago Theological Seminary recognized his unusual energy and his leadership qualities. They worked closely with him to make sure he got the most from his studies. One professor remembers him as "a young man eager to learn everything he could as fast as he could."

Having a family did not slow Jesse down. Besides doing his schoolwork, he found odd jobs to support the family. Jacqueline helped pay bills by working at the seminary's library. She and the wives of other students took turns caring for one another's children during working hours.

Jesse's athletic skills were put to good use at the seminary. It was a small school, sharing a campus with the large University of Chicago. Before Jesse came, the seminary's teams had competed poorly with the university's teams. With Jesse on the basketball, baseball, and football teams, the seminary soon became intramural champion.

In his usual way, Jesse found time for sports, for his family, and for his studies. He was still striving to excel in all things. As he studied the Bible, Jesse saw it as a history of the Jewish people fighting for their freedom. It seemed to him that the Bible described a series of civil rights struggles.

Jesse joined the Southern Christian Leadership Conference (SCLC) in Chicago, and he continued to follow the civil rights struggle of his own time. Leading that struggle was Dr. Martin Luther King, Jr., president of the SCLC. The purpose of the SCLC was to fight all forms of segregation and to increase voter registration. Dr. King vowed to keep all protests nonviolent.

By 1964, Martin Luther King, Jr., and the SCLC had made great progress in the South. Still, blacks in many places could not register to vote. When they tried to register, they were kept standing in line for hours. Then they were told the registration office was closed.

Toward the end of 1964, the SCLC began a campaign for voter registration in Selma, Alabama. Its peaceful protests ended with police violence. In February 1965, Dr. King was arrested for leading a march in Selma. Not discouraged, he organized another march after his release from prison. This time the protesters would walk from Selma to Montgomery, the capital of Alabama. Dr. King wanted a voting rights law that would make sure voters could register.

Alabama's governor, George Wallace, sent out state troopers armed with guns to keep the demonstrators from marching. Dr. King was determined to defy the governor. He called for supporters everywhere to join the march from Selma.

From Chicago, Jesse Jackson watched television reports about the protest movement in Selma. He saw the brutal way the police treated demonstrators. When Dr. King called for help, Jesse organized half the students from the seminary. They drove all night in a caravan of automobiles to reach Selma in time. They thought about the dangers ahead.

One of Jesse's professors, Dr. Howard Schomer, had flown from Chicago to be with Dr. King. As he joined the procession in Selma, he ran into the group of students from his seminary, led by Jesse Jackson. All were wearing minister's white collars. Dr. Schomer growled at them: "What are you all doing inside those clerical collars? I never saw one of you wear a clerical collar before!" Jesse called back, "Take it easy, Doc. We don't have any gray hair to protect us, like you."

People from all over the country responded to Dr. King's call for help. President Lyndon Johnson sent federal troops to protect the marchers. Eventually, about fifty thousand people, half of them white, made their way into Montgomery. In August 1965, the Voting Rights Act was made into law.

The man they had all come to support, Martin Luther King, Jr., was Jesse's hero. In Chicago, as a member of the SCLC, Jesse had spoken many times on Dr. King's behalf. In Greensboro, he had been one of many students attending Dr. King's nonviolence workshops. Yet, Jesse had never come face-to-face with the civil rights leader.

At Selma, Jesse had a chance to work directly with Dr. King for the first time. He came to respect Dr. King more than ever. He admired his wisdom and the way he expressed himself, and his coolness in the face of danger. He said,

"King was like a giant . . . he was not afraid of violence and bullets and bombs."

Dr. King and the staff members of the SCLC were impressed and surprised by Jesse Jackson. He was willing to work hard, no matter how small the task. He did not mind going out in the rain to bring coffee back for the staff, or running any number of errands. On the other hand, some staffers thought he could be too forward. Sometimes he gave orders without being directed to do so, or acted without consulting the staff.

Many people were surprised one day in March 1965, when Jesse climbed the steps outside Brown Chapel in Selma and joined the SCLC leaders to give a speech. No one had invited him to talk. It upset some staff people to see an inexperienced, twenty-three-year-old student taking over that way. Jesse's old love for attention and need to feel important seemed to push him forward.

Jesse's words, however, deeply affected the large crowd gathered on the pavement below. Newspaper and television stories praised the talk given by the unknown young man. Reporters noted his rough work clothes and the funny hat he wore over his close-cropped hair.

When the marching and speech making were over, Jesse stopped at a gas station to call home. Jacqueline was expecting their second child and had not been able to go with him to Selma. He learned on the phone that she had given birth to a son, Jesse, Junior.

After the victory in Selma, Dr. King turned his attention to the terrible living conditions in city ghettos in the North and West. Chicago was among his first targets, because its large ghettos were splitting at the seams. Almost as many

blacks lived in Chicago's poor and crowded slums as in all
of the state of Mississippi.

Al Raby, a leader of the Coordinating Council of Community Organizations (CCCO), invited Dr. King to come
to Chicago. Jesse Jackson was in a position to be helpful.
On his return from Alabama, Jesse had continued to work
for the SCLC in Chicago. He was also a part of the CCCO,
a league of neighborhood civil rights groups.

Before Dr. King's arrival, the SCLC and the CCCO
united under the name of the Chicago Freedom Movement.
Their goals were to bring about equal opportunities for
blacks and to help them find better jobs and better housing.
They planned nonviolent sit-ins and marches.

In preparing for Dr. King's arrival, Jackson had the
job of organizing Chicago's black community. It was not an
easy job, because many poor people were afraid of new
ideas and change. Ghetto dwellers in Chicago understood
the political power of their mayor, Richard J. Daley. If they
voted his way during an election, they might be rewarded
with a job or a better apartment, or a chicken for their
dinner. It was risky to offend the mayor by asking for their
rights. They might lose their public housing or welfare
benefits.

Knowing the influence black ministers had on their
followers, Jesse Jackson tried to reach people through their
churches. At first, the ministers did not trust the bold young
student who talked of civil rights. They, too, feared that life
would be harder for black people if they did not please the
white political bosses.

One minister, the Reverend Clay Evans, offered to help.
He liked Jesse's self-confidence and wanted to join forces

with Dr. King. Clay Evans was in the process of building a new church for his congregation. The foundation was in place, and so were the steel girders to support the roof. But the mayor's staff heard that Evans was supporting King, and they kept the minister from getting the loan he needed to complete the building. They told him, "If you get out of the civil rights movement, you can have the money."

Clay Evans was not discouraged. He would manage without the new church building. "The real church is in the heart of the people," he said. "No one can stop me there—no political party, no mayor, no governor." The steel posts remained standing for seven years, until the church was finally built.

Before long, Jesse Jackson won the support of the ministers of other large churches. They and their followers began to see the importance of fighting for civil rights. What's more, Clay Evans took Jackson into his Fellowship Baptist Church as youth minister.

In January of 1966, Martin Luther King, Jr., came to Chicago with his wife and four children. Jesse Jackson met them at the airport, driving a limousine furnished by his new church. Dr. King was pleased with the progress of the Chicago Freedom Movement and with Jackson's success in organizing the black community. The two men worked together during Dr. King's stay in the city.

News reporters followed on the heels of Dr. King and the Chicago Freedom workers. Sometimes Jesse talked to the press alone, and he discovered that he enjoyed those opportunities. Perhaps at those times he felt he truly had become somebody.

A number of times Jesse made public statements without checking with Dr. King or other senior staff people. Dr. King was patient and tried to correct mistakes Jesse made. He gave him advice and helped prepare him for leadership. They discussed important books and ideas. Jesse found in Dr. King a father, a brother, and a teacher.

To call attention to the dreadful living conditions in Chicago's slums, Dr. King and his family moved into a West Side apartment. The flat was run-down and dirty and filled with trash. The hall had no lights and smelled bad. When newspapers published the address of Dr. King's apartment, the building suddenly filled with plumbers, carpenters, and painters, making repairs and cleaning up.

However, Dr. King could not move from building to building to put an end to all of Chicago's slums. Instead, he began holding workshops on nonviolence for young people. Many former gang members joined Dr. King's movement.

In July of 1966, Dr. King conducted a massive rally at Soldiers Field in Chicago. Jesse Jackson helped organize the rally and the march that followed from Soldiers Field to city hall. At city hall, Dr. King presented a list of demands to Chicago's mayor, Richard Daley. The list included a number of basic rights for blacks, but the chief demand was to end the city's slums and to open up white neighborhoods to blacks. Mayor Daley rejected the demands.

Dr. King's next move was to lead marches into Chicago's white neighborhoods. Again, Jesse Jackson helped organize the marches. Many of the protesters were white, marching in sympathy with the black people. Nuns and priests were also among the marchers.

The white residents were furious—the police had to keep them on one side of the street and the protesters on the other. Still, the police could not prevent violence. In one neighborhood, cars belonging to some protesters were pushed into a nearby lagoon or burned. On one occasion, Dr. King was hurt when he was hit by a rock. During another march, Jesse Jackson's head was split open with a brick thrown from the mob. There might have been more injuries, if not for young blacks with baseball mitts who caught the flying bricks and threw them back.

More violence followed, in black communities as well as in white neighborhoods. People in both communities were angry at Mayor Daley, and he began to worry about losing the next election. Finally, he was ready to listen to the demands of the black people.

In August 1966, Mayor Daley called a meeting to solve the city's problems. Jesse Jackson and other local leaders went with Dr. King to the meeting. Mayor Daley promised to put an end to slums in Chicago if Dr. King called off the marches. Dr. King agreed. The mayor drew up a pact, promising to end Chicago's housing discrimination and to allow blacks to live in any neighborhood they chose. Seeing this as a victory, Dr. King signed the agreement and made plans to move his family back to the South. However, when King left the city, the mayor failed to keep his word.

Before leaving the city, Dr. King appointed Jesse Jackson director of the Chicago branch of the SCLC's Operation Breadbasket. One of the chief aims of this project was to create more jobs for black people. Jesse saw the work with Operation Breadbasket as a great challenge. It was an opportunity to help his people improve their living conditions.

In the thick of the housing struggle, Jesse had stopped going to classes at the seminary. His professors expected him to come back when the fight was over. But Jesse was eager to begin his job. He was forced to make a difficult decision. Although it was only a few months until graduation, he dropped out of the seminary.

Jesse Jackson did not graduate with his class, but the Chicago Theological Seminary gave him an honorary degree three years later, in June of 1969.

Chapter/Five

"... Black pocketbook power."

At the age of twenty-four, Jesse Jackson was director of the Chicago branch of Operation Breadbasket. Three white ministry students came to work with him. Their first "office" was in the apartment where Jesse Jackson and his family lived. By this time there were three children in the family. The youngest, Jonathan Luther, was born in Chicago and named for Martin Luther King, Jr. The staff members made their way past the baby in his playpen, and past the other children and their toys, before starting their meetings. Later they had a real office.

The goal of Operation Breadbasket was to create jobs for black people and to help black-owned businesses. The name was Dr. King's brainchild. It was a good name for a program that brought bread and income into the baskets of poor people. The idea for the program came from Dr. Leon Sullivan, a black minister who had started a similar project in Philadelphia. With Dr. Sullivan's help, Dr. King had set up the first Operation Breadbasket for the Southern Christian Leadership Conference in Atlanta, Georgia.

The Chicago branch opened four years later, in 1966. Under Jackson, the program became a huge success. Later, branches were set up in cities across the country, with Jesse Jackson as the national director.

When Operation Breadbasket opened in Chicago, Jackson followed the plan that had worked well in Philadelphia and Atlanta. First, he asked black people to buy products made by black-owned companies and to shop at black-owned stores. If they did so, their money would stay in their own community, where it was needed.

Second, he asked white-owned businesses that made a profit from black customers to change their policies. He called for equal job opportunities for black people. He also asked stores to make room on their shelves for products made by black companies.

At that time, Chicago's black population was over a million people. They spent more than $4 billion each year in the city's shops and offices. Yet, many stores in the black communities did not hire blacks, except for a few low-paying jobs. No blacks were driving trucks that delivered soft drinks, ice cream, or bread. Banks and insurance companies did not hire black office workers.

One hundred black ministers helped Jackson carry out the plan to create more jobs. Their first success came with Country Delight, a dairy chain that owned 104 stores in ghetto neighborhoods. When the dairy refused to hire black workers, the ministers called on their church members to boycott the dairy—to not buy milk and other products made by Country Delight.

As the boycott began, people formed picket lines in front

of stores selling Country Delight products. They carried signs asking shoppers not to buy groceries there. At one point, thugs hired by the store owners threatened to kill Jesse Jackson. He ignored the threats, and the boycott continued.

Since it carried items that spoil easily, such as milk and butter, the dairy lost money each day the boycott continued. With cartons piling up on the store shelves, Country Delight soon agreed to Operation Breadbasket's terms. Three days after the boycott began, Country Delight hired forty-four black workers and began training black drivers for its delivery trucks.

Using the same plan, Operation Breadbasket had one success after another. Within a few months, major dairies, soft drink companies, and grocery chain stores were hiring hundreds of blacks for jobs in Chicago's ghetto. Many stores did not wait for Operation Breadbasket to threaten them with boycotts. They gave in because, as Jackson says, "they heard our footsteps coming."

One reporter wrote that Chicago businesspeople "have learned the hard way that Jesse Jackson is no country preacher. They have felt the black pocketbook power of his Operation Breadbasket."

The Atlantic & Pacific Tea Company (A&P) was one of Chicago's oldest and largest grocery chains. It operated forty stores in the ghetto. When A&P signed an agreement with Operation Breadbasket in 1967, it promised to add 770 new jobs for blacks. A year later, Breadbasket staff members discovered that A&P had not kept its word. At that point, A&P said it had no intention of carrying out its promise.

Operation Breadbasket returned to boycotting. This time the white community helped. Hundreds of white customers refused to shop at A&P stores. They formed picket lines in their own neighborhoods, in sympathy with blacks. During a three-month battle, A&P lost about $10 million. Finally, it gave in and signed a new agreement with Operation Breadbasket. The second time, the A&P Company kept its word.

Besides hiring more black workers, A&P agreed to use black businesses for advertising, construction work, trash removal, and exterminating. A&P also promised to make room on its shelves for black-made products. This meant that shoppers could choose items such as Joe Louis milk, Staff of Life bread, Mumbo barbecue sauce, and Grove Fresh orange juice.

Jackson once explained to a group of women in his church why they should buy black products. He said, "Now, Joe Louis milk does not come from a Negro cow. That milk has 400 units of Vitamin D like any other milk. It's written right there on the carton. Only difference is that your husband can make twelve thousand dollars a year driving a truck for this company."

Jackson also wanted to make black banks stronger. The banks needed enough money to make loans for putting up buildings, for improving homes and businesses, and for backing scholarships. Jackson asked government officials in Illinois to deposit public funds in black banks. Mayor Daley and the county treasurer refused. However, State Treasurer Adlai Stevenson III deposited large sums of state money into two black banks in Chicago.

Black Christmas and Black Easter were two other ideas

that helped black merchants. The Christmas idea was first thought of by another community leader, Robert Lucas. He suggested that black people boycott stores in downtown Chicago during the Christmas season.

Jackson took the idea a few steps further. He urged people to buy gift items that were made by blacks or sold by black-owned shops. "Rather than looking through the yellow pages, you've got to start looking through the black pages," he said. Parents were asked to open savings accounts for their children in black banks. People who could afford it were urged to invite poor black families to their homes for Christmas dinner.

The first Black Christmas in Chicago was celebrated in 1968. It was already December when the idea of a parade came to Jackson. Immediately he phoned friends, Operation Breadbasket staff members, businesspeople, and politicians. He wanted to be sure there would be plenty of floats, marching units, music, entertainment, and publicity.

With ninety floats, the parade was a huge success. There was no bearded, white Saint Nick—the star was a jolly, black Soul Saint from the South Pole. A friend of Jackson stuffed a pillow under his black dashiki (a loose-fitting, pullover garment) to play the role.

The following spring, Jackson started a Black Easter program. Another parade was planned, and this time the star was a woolly black sheep. The floats were decorated to honor black heroes, such as Malcolm X, Dr. Martin Luther King, Jr., Paul Laurence Dunbar, and William E. B. Du Bois. If people planned to get new clothing and bonnets for Easter, Jackson urged them to buy from black merchants. He reminded them that "buying black" would keep their money in the black community, where it would be used for their benefit.

The success of Black Christmas and Black Easter soon led to a yearly trade fair, put on by Jackson and the SCLC. Businesspeople who benefited from Operation Breadbasket were happy to supply the money to operate the fairs. Known as Black Expos, the fairs were held in Chicago's large Amphitheater. Hundreds of black companies displayed their products and services, and took orders for future sales.

The fairs attracted teenagers, adults, and families, who were willing to pay a fee to attend. Besides the business taking place, there were cultural events. The walls were often hung with bright, modern art, along with pictures of famous black Americans. There were treats for children, as well as live entertainment that included well-known black singers, black comedians, and popular black bands. Thousands of black and white people mingled as they examined the displays and enjoyed the performances.

Many of Jesse Jackson's ideas had been first expressed while he was a student at the Chicago Theological Seminary. He had been allowed to use the school's dining room to talk with a few black ministers about civil rights on Saturday mornings. The Saturday morning meetings continued after Operation Breadbasket was formed and Jackson left the seminary. Businesspeople and other leaders soon began coming to the meetings, where they could discuss common problems and solutions.

Before long, people from all walks of life—bankers, taxi drivers, business owners, and garbage removers—were coming to the Saturday gatherings. Spouses were invited, and coffee and doughnuts were served.

By 1968, the meetings outgrew the seminary and were moved to the Capitol Theater on the South Side. When Jesse Jackson became a minister that year, the Capitol Theater became his "church." Each Saturday, a gospel band played music and a choir sang at the service. His sermons were broadcast regularly over the radio. At home and in the church, the audience heard about the latest Operation Breadbasket activities.

During these Saturday meetings, the Reverend Jesse Jackson urged people to take pride in their blackness. As the music swelled and people clapped and swayed, he called out to the audience, "I am Somebody," and they called back, "I am Somebody." He chanted, "I am black—beautiful—proud!" The audience chanted back, "I am black—beautiful—proud!"

Early in 1968, Jesse Jackson, along with other SCLC aides, worked with Dr. Martin Luther King, Jr., in planning a march to Washington, D.C. They called it the Poor People's Campaign. The plan was for people of all races to come to the nation's capitol. It was a way of getting Congress to pay attention to the great number of poor and jobless people in the country.

Thousands of poor people marched into Washington in May of 1968. For six weeks they camped in the park next to the Lincoln Memorial. They called the camp Resurrection City, and Jackson was named city manager. He kept the protesters calm, in spite of fights among themselves and constant rains that put the camp deep in mud. When a flu epidemic started, the people were forced to leave.

Before leaving, Jackson led a group of marchers to a government cafeteria, where they ran up a lunch bill of almost three hundred dollars. Jackson refused to pay the bill, saying it was a small part of what the nation owed the poor.

The SCLC leaders conducted the Poor People's Campaign without the person who had helped plan the event. Early in April, Dr. King had been called to Memphis, Tennessee, where trouble had started. Garbage collectors there were on strike because of unfair treatment. Both the police and the strikers used violence, and Dr. King came to carry out a peaceful march. The night after he arrived, April 4, 1968, as he stood on the balcony of his motel room, Dr. Martin Luther King, Jr. was shot by an assassin. He was rushed to the hospital, but died within the hour.

Jesse Jackson and other SCLC staff members were in Memphis with Dr. King that night. They were shocked and grief stricken.

Mourning the loss to himself and to the country, Jesse Jackson had returned home. Arriving in Chicago, he found the West Side ghetto in flames. News of Dr. King's death had sent waves of violence through the community. Angry blacks set fire to stores and buildings owned by both blacks and whites. They attacked firefighters trying to put out the blaze.

Jesse Jackson pleaded with the people not to be violent. He reminded them that they would show their faith in Dr. King by putting down their rocks and their bottles.

Before it was over, nine black people were dead and one thousand were left homeless.

The day after Dr. King's death, Chicago's mayor, Richard J. Daley, had called a special session of the city council to honor the black leader. Jesse Jackson addressed the council in anger. Dark glasses hid his sleepless eyes, and he was dressed in the same clothes he had worn in Memphis the day before. He reminded the mayor and the council of how badly they behaved when Dr. King was in Chicago. He said, "A fitting memorial to Dr. King would be not to sit here looking sad and pious, but to behave differently."

After Dr. King's death, Jesse Jackson took on a new position of leadership. It was seen at the Operation Breadbasket memorial service for Dr. King. The Saturday before Dr. King's death, four hundred people had come to the meeting. For his memorial service, four thousand people showed up.

Chapter/Six

" . . . To serve humanity."

A few months after Dr. King's death, Jesse Jackson was ordained a minister at the Fellowship Baptist Church. Jacqueline Jackson watched the ceremony with pride. Her husband looked dignified in his black robe. Santita, Jesse, Junior, and Jonathan Luther had trouble sitting still. They thought the ceremony would never end.

By the end of 1968, the Reverend Jesse Jackson was well known across the nation. As national director of Operation Breadbasket, he gave talks and supervised its affairs in sixteen different cities. Flying back and forth, he returned to Chicago for the Saturday morning meetings.

His handsome appearance and commanding voice attracted large audiences wherever he spoke. Long ago he had given up the neat suit and tie he once preferred. Instead, he wore turtleneck sweaters and leather vests or dashikis and bell-bottomed trousers. They looked good with his big Afro and drooping moustache. He also wore a medallion with the image of Dr. Martin Luther King, Jr., on it.

Whether he addressed people with no education or those who were well educated, Jackson spoke a language his audience understood. He could switch from street talk to more worldly speech with great ease. A razor-sharp memory and a booming voice added to his talents as a speaker. He stretched his arms and waved his hands to make a point. He was popular with audiences everywhere.

In December of that year his travels were interrupted by an unexpected stay in the hospital. It came about during a campaign in Chicago to get more construction jobs for blacks. While demonstrating in front of a building under construction, he and four others were arrested and sent to jail. When he became sick, Jackson was taken from the jail to the hospital.

Doctors found that he was suffering from sickle-cell trait, a blood disease affecting mostly black people whose ancestors came from West Africa. Sickle-cell trait protects people from malaria, but it lowers their resistance to more common illnesses. With his usual humor, Jesse Jackson welcomed an African disease. Anyone could have the flu or pneumonia, but for sickle-cell trait, one had to be black.

Spending several weeks in the hospital did not keep him from Operation Breadbasket business. He held press conferences in the hospital lounge. Or, propped up in bed, he led business discussions in his room. Other times he left the hospital to attend important meetings or to deliver his Saturday morning talk. Afterwards, he returned to bed.

While in the hospital, he was pleased to learn that the protest at the construction site had been successful. The labor unions had agreed to hire and train four thousand black workers.

The following year, 1969, Jackson was pleased by another event. His half brother Noah Robinson, Jr., came to Chicago to work with him. Noah had been studying business in graduate school, at the University of Pennsylvania, when Jackson asked him to join Operation Breadbasket. With Noah in charge of the business department, Operation Breadbasket became even more successful.

A year later, however, the two men quarreled. Noah left the organization and began his own business. Since then, the brothers have patched up their differences, but Noah has continued in business for himself.

In 1971, Jackson resigned from Operation Breadbasket and the Southern Christian Leadership Conference. For some time there had been tension between him and the SCLC staff in Atlanta. When Dr. King died, Dr. Ralph D. Abernathy became the new SCLC director. The staff had expected Dr. Abernathy to become national leader of the civil rights movement. However, Jackson's popularity seemed to put him in the position of leadership.

The final break between Jackson and the SCLC came after the Black Expo of 1971. Abernathy learned that Jackson had set up the trade fair independently, instead of under the SCLC. It was rumored that Jackson had not properly shared the profits of the expo with the SCLC.

Dr. Abernathy came to Chicago with a committee of staff members to face Jackson. When they examined the records of the fair, they could find no evidence of dishonesty. Nevertheless, Abernathy suspended him for sixty days for taking the Black Expo away from the SCLC. Jackson promptly resigned and formed his own organization, Operation PUSH.

At first, the letters in the name PUSH stood for People United to Save Humanity. One of the ministers in the group, the Reverend Alvin Pitcher, thought the word *serve* was a better choice than the word *save*. Humanity could not be saved, he reminded them, by mere humans. Several years later, PUSH changed its name to People United to Serve Humanity.

When Jackson left the SCLC, the Saturday morning meetings moved with him—choir, band, radio broadcast, and all. At first they met in an old, drafty theater. Later, Operation PUSH bought its own building, a former synagogue on Chicago's South Side, and the rallies continued in the new auditorium. Its high ceiling and stained glass windows added to the religious tone of the meetings.

Operation PUSH's goals were close to those of Operation Breadbasket's, but there were some changes. By 1971, the battle for basic civil rights had been won. Blacks could no longer be denied service in restaurants, stores, or hotels because of their color. The next fight would be for economic rights—the right to compete in the business world.

Jackson's new program called for better jobs, good medical care, quality education, and improved living conditions for blacks. High on the list of goals was providing more opportunities for black businesses to grow.

In the years that followed, Operation PUSH worked with major businesses all over the country to achieve those goals. General Foods, one of the nation's largest corporations, was among PUSH's early successes. (Jell-O, Kool-Aid, Grapenuts cereal, and Birdseye frozen foods are among the many products General Foods makes.) An agreement General Foods signed with PUSH provided hundreds of jobs for blacks and other minorities. General Foods also agreed to hire black doctors and lawyers for its special needs. Further, it promised to place $20 million of its insurance with black insurance companies and to deposit large sums of money into black banks.

Operation PUSH worked out similar deals with other national corporations. Kentucky Fried Chicken, Burger King, Seven-Up, and Ford Motor Company are only a few of the companies that signed agreements.

Companies that were slow in coming to terms with PUSH found themselves in an awkward position. For example, when the Coca-Cola Company hesitated, Jackson asked PUSH members to drink less of that product. Their slogan became Don't Choke on Coke. It was not an official boycott, but two weeks later Coca-Cola signed an agreement.

Later, Jackson and PUSH worked with foreign companies doing business in the United States. They tried to set up outlets among black businesses in the United States for selling automobiles and other products made overseas.

Over the years, many critics have found fault with Jackson's support of black business. They say he has helped people who are already better off than most. Some businesspeople have become millionaires as a result of PUSH's programs. Critics have complained that Jackson has not done enough for the poor.

Jackson reminds his critics that what serves the black business community serves all black people—rich, poor, and middle class. As black businesses prosper, they provide more jobs for blacks. As poor blacks earn more money and improve their lives, they usually seek more education. Jackson believes that when poor people join the middle class, they may provide new leadership in the black community.

Jackson also reminds his critics that poor people have always been his concern. Not long after the Poor People's Campaign in Washington, D.C., he led a hunger drive in Illinois. At that time the state legislature was going to vote on a bill that would cut about fifteen dollars each month from welfare payments to the poor. Jackson was outraged. "This is open war against poor people," he said.

In May of 1969, he arranged for about two thousand people to march into Springfield, the state capital, to protest the bill. He met with the governor and gave a sermon to Illinois lawmakers about the problems of the poor. As he spoke, he raised his voice and pounded on the table. The bill was not passed. In addition, Jackson's efforts brought about a plan that provided free lunch for needy children.

More recently, he and PUSH called attention to "the poorest county in the United States," Tunica County, Mississippi. The town of Tunica had no streets, only alleys. Families lived along a smelly drainage canal they called Sugar Ditch. The unpainted houses had leaking roofs, rotting floors, cracked walls, and no indoor plumbing. Many people paid between twenty-five and eighty-five dollars a month to live there.

Tunica's population of nearly ten thousand people included seven thousand blacks. More than half the people suffered from extreme poverty and hunger. Unemployment was high, and there were no job opportunities. Jackson called Tunica "our national shame."

Operation PUSH "adopted" Tunica in 1985 and began raising funds to help the people. Jackson brought a delegation of state representatives and ministers to inspect the county. Within a few months, families were moved from their old shacks into house trailers. The new housing was provided by the state of Mississippi, with the help of the U.S. government. In time, Jackson also hoped to improve the residents' health, their education, and their political strength. He said, "We must keep challenging our nation to focus on poverty."

Fighting first for civil rights and then for economic rights, the Reverend Jesse Jackson has always stood for human rights. Individuals have been as important as groups. PUSH has helped veterans, welfare mothers, and unemployed workers collect benefits. It has aided victims of fire disasters and families facing eviction notices—as well as victims of the justice system.

In Chicago, a bus driver was involved in a serious accident. His bus collided with an automobile filled with young people on their way to a rock concert. All of the automobile's occupants were killed. Many witnesses came forward to testify that the bus driver was not at fault, yet the state's attorney held him responsible for the deaths. After Jackson spoke in the driver's defense, the state's attorney reexamined the case, and the charges were dropped.

Across the nation, PUSH has fought for improvements in employment, education, health, voter registration, politics, women's rights, and the law. When a shortage of oil created an energy crisis in the 1970s, Jackson gave support to workers whose jobs were threatened. He helped develop a network of ministers in many cities to work toward making unions stronger to protect the workers. When farmers in Illinois worried about losing their farms, Jackson went to

Springfield to address state senators and representatives. He urged them to pass a new law to keep farmers from losing their land.

In working out business deals with PUSH, large companies have been urged to make donations to black schools. These donations have made it possible for universities and colleges to expand their programs and to offer scholarships to needy students.

Keeping people healthy has been a special interest of Jesse Jackson. In 1974, he was given an award by the American Public Health Association for his "concern for the total health and well-being of all people." The award recognized two programs established by Jackson. He had set up nutrition programs in many American communities and supervised the quality and cost of foods sold in neighborhood stores. And drought and famine in Africa had moved him to organize a campaign to deliver food and medical supplies to West African countries.

Other awards and honors have been bestowed on Jesse Jackson over the years. Honorary degrees have been given to him by many colleges and universities. He has appeared often on television news and talk shows, and his photograph has been on the covers of magazines. Thousands of articles have been written about him. But perhaps no honor has meant as much as the celebration in his hometown on October 6, 1973.

In Greenville, South Carolina, Jesse Jackson Day was celebrated with a weekend of festivities. Townspeople, white and black, greeted him with pride and affection. Many wore medallions with his image. Signs were posted in store windows and on hotel fronts, reading, "Welcome Home,

Reverend Jesse Jackson." The *Greenville-Piedmont News* printed a full-page greeting: "Here Comes the Son."

Friends and followers came by automobile, train, and plane to honor him. The governor and other public officials sent telegrams of congratulations. Reporters and photographers were there to cover the event. Wherever he went that weekend, Jackson was accompanied by the sheriff's car, its lights flashing and the siren wailing. The sheriff's bodyguards never let him out of their sight.

At the main banquet, speakers stood up to praise the man. There were tears in Jesse Jackson's eyes as he spoke to the guests who honored him. He had come a long way since his boyhood in Greenville, but so had the town, the South, and the entire nation. In the view of many people, he had truly become somebody.

Chapter/Seven

" . . . Up with hope."

A year later, in 1974, Jackson's luck turned bad. He developed pneumonia, complicated by the sickle-cell trait. It took five long stays in the hospital to recover.

There were also financial problems in PUSH. The organization owed large sums of money. In addition, the government suspected some wrongdoing and began checking PUSH's records. Although the government found nothing wrong, the suspicion was upsetting to Jackson.

To make matters worse, the yearly trade fair (now called PUSH Expo) had to be cancelled. A drop in business in 1973 and 1974 had caused losses all over the United States. In Chicago, almost half of the black-owned businesses had closed down. As business declined, businesspeople hesitated to invest money in PUSH Expo—they had less to spend and they knew fewer buyers would attend the fair. Also, some staff members complained that PUSH's business department was losing customers because it was not keeping in touch with them.

There were other complaints from the PUSH staff about the way PUSH was run, and a number of people resigned. Some black aides resented white staff members. They wanted PUSH to succeed without the help of white people. It did not matter that several white ministers had been with the group since it began as Operation Breadbasket.

Other aides, black and white, were unhappy for different reasons. Many felt that Jackson gave them a great deal of responsibility but not enough authority. When it was time to make a decision, they had to go to him for the final word. One by one, important staff members began to leave PUSH. Among those who resigned were the associate director and several top assistants who had worked with Jackson for many years.

Late in 1974, Jackson went to Kansas City, Missouri, to lead a Baptist revival meeting. He fasted and prayed for guidance. A few weeks later, he felt his prayers were answered.

On the birthday of Martin Luther King, Jr., January 15, 1975, Jackson led a march in Washington, D.C. Thousands of people came to call attention to the masses of jobless people in the country. The plan was to march around the White House seven times, but many marchers did not make it. As people dropped out, Jackson noticed that many were on drugs and could barely walk. He said, "It occurred to me then that no general can win a war with a drunk army."

A short time earlier he had had a similar reaction when he drove past a Chicago school. He was horrified to see kids sitting outside, during school hours, smoking and shooting dice. He was also dismayed to see that five of the girls were pregnant.

Those two incidents caused Jackson to change the direction of PUSH. Instead of concentrating on business, he would turn to education. He would fight the evil of drugs and other bad habits that kept young people from becoming healthy, intelligent adults. He called his new project PUSH for Excellence, or Project EXCEL.

For the next two years he traveled from high school to high school, taking his message to several large cities. Many of the schools were in black ghettos. As he walked onto the stage, wearing a trim business suit and a tie, the students took notice of his athletic bearing and his self-confidence. He was already a hero to many, and when he talked about the dangers of drugs and alcohol, they sat up and listened.

He understood the problems teenagers faced. They needed help in developing a better sense of their own worth. He combined his famous I Am Somebody message with "Down with dope and up with hope."

He knew that poor children often had no hope of ever moving out of their bad situations. He gave them hope by saying they could change their lives if they had the will. "Work hard and strive for excellence," he said. "You may be in the slums, but don't let the slums be in you."

Boys in many schools were in the habit of wearing their hats in class. At one school they might wear colored knit hats; at another, they wore broad-brimmed hats. The hats seemed to be symbols of their boldness and power. Teachers could not persuade the boys to remove them inside the school. When Jackson came to these schools, he was polite but firm. He used the street talk students understood, and they paid sharp attention. When he asked them to remove their hats, one by one, the hats came off.

He told students they would do as well in class as in sports if they took their hats off in school and turned their television sets off at home. He said, "If you spend two hours a night learning to read and write, you'll be able to slam dunk a thought the way you slam dunk a basketball."

At a school in Chicago, Jackson called the captain of the basketball team to the stage. He asked, "If you're behind in the game, what do you do?" The captain said, "Try harder." Jackson replied, "It's the same in the game of life."

At each school, Jackson asked students to sign a pledge for excellence. The pledge called for promises not to deal in drugs and alcohol, and to study two hours a night.

Parents made pledges, too. As a father, Jackson knew that when parents showed interest in their children's schoolwork, students performed better. Yet parents often did not follow their children's progress. Many of these parents were shocked to learn that their children had reached the eighth grade without learning to read or write. In Jackson's program, parents pledged to meet with their children's teachers the first week of school and to keep in touch all year. At home they were to see that children studied at least two hours a night, without the radio, television, or telephone. Parents were also asked to pick up their children's report cards personally and to keep track of their test scores.

Teachers pledged to call parents if students were absent two days in a row or if they were having trouble with their schoolwork. Principals pledged to set firm goals and rules and to be sure that students understood them. Jackson suggested that rules be set for proper dress and that students come to school with pride and dignity.

Many of the high schools Jackson visited were in bad condition. Windows were cracked or broken, walls were covered with graffiti, and equipment was frequently stolen. In some cities, police were assigned to keep students from fighting with their fists or with knives.

At a school in Los Angeles, almost half the students were absent on Fridays, and came late the rest of the week. Once Project EXCEL got under way, changes began to take place. Fewer students were absent and there was very little tardiness. At the same time, less fighting and violence occurred. Jackson said, "People simply changed their minds about themselves."

What helped turn those students around were talks about the way athletes trained. Jackson explained that serious athletes spent weeks practicing and gave up many pleasures in order to do so. Their hard work and careful discipline led them to excel. Whether they were Olympic stars or champion boxers or high school athletes, their respect for discipline was the reason they succeeded. The same was true for students who wanted to be doctors or lawyers or anything else.

At the same school in Los Angeles, students decided to make their school Number One in academics as well as in sports. About two hundred students formed a PUSH for Excellence club that concentrated on math and history and held sex education conferences. One group of students in Kansas City, Missouri, raised money to carpet the auditorium, paint murals on the walls, and plant trees.

By 1977, Jackson had brought Project EXCEL to a number of schools in Chicago, Los Angeles, and Kansas City. One Sunday evening, the television show "Sixty

Minutes" broadcast a description of the project. Among those watching the show that day were Hubert Humphrey, a former vice-president of the United States, and Joseph Califano, head of the nation's education department. The next day, Humphrey telephoned Califano and arranged for Jackson to receive a grant of government money to take his project to more schools.

A number of schools already had their own programs that encouraged students to take their studies seriously. They, too, worked for more cooperation between parents and teachers. When Jackson came to these schools, they folded his ideas into their own programs. One Chicago principal with his own program found that his students were inspired all over again when Jackson came to talk.

Under the PUSH for Excellence system, thousands of graduating seniors also registered to vote. When students finished four years of high school, they received not only a diploma, but a voter's registration card. Along with the card were instructions on operating voting machines and information on the election process.

Not everyone thought the project was good. Some teachers and principals felt it was unfair to expect poor blacks to improve their own situations. So many had been born into a life of troubles. For long years before the civil rights movement, black people had been kept from improving their lives. The critics said that these people needed much more help in solving their problems. They were victims of a bad system.

Jackson felt that by taking the first steps themselves, students would grow confident about changing their lives. He said, "The victim is not responsible for being down, but he is responsible for getting up." After all, Jackson knew what it was like to grow up in hard times. He had not forgotten his boyhood in Greenville, South Carolina. By hard work and discipline, he had helped himself to overcome many disadvantages.

Other critics complained that the project was not well organized. Students were inspired when Jackson spoke to them, but after he left, there was no program to keep things going. But it was a movement, not a program, Jackson explained. He talked of the hundreds of young people who wrote letters to him and spoke to him on the street. He said, "They tell me how they were going to drop out or give up. Then they remembered something I had said that inspired them not to drop out or not to give up."

In spite of the critics, PUSH for Excellence met with much praise. Within a few years Jackson received between $2 million and $3 million in contributions to take the project to more schools in more cities. The money came from government agencies and from private groups, such as the Ford Foundation, the Rockefeller Fund, and CBS.

These funds started him on a new round of travels and talks. In most schools Jackson was greeted by cheering students and teachers. Once again his name made frequent news headlines.

By 1981, Operation PUSH was a huge organization with a large staff. PUSH for Excellence was registered as a separate corporation. When the government demanded to know how its grants had been spent, it discovered that PUSH had not kept clear records. PUSH could not prove where all the money had gone.

After the government examined PUSH's records, the

organization returned over seven hundred thousand dollars from grants received earlier. For a while, the license to operate PUSH for Excellence was taken away. Later the license was reissued, and PUSH continued as a corporation in good standing. When the investigation was over, PUSH announced it no longer wished to receive government funds for its educational project. After that, money for the project came from the PUSH-EXCEL Professional Basketball Classic played each year, as well as from private persons and businesses.

Jesse Jackson continued to fly across the country, inspiring school groups with hope. Almost everywhere he was greeted as a superstar. With PUSH for Excellence running smoothly again, he turned his attention to world affairs.

Chapter/Eight

"Jesse Jetstream."

When Jesse Jackson had been studying to be a minister, he learned about the problems of other countries. A United Nations ambassador from Lebanon had visited the Chicago Theological Seminary one evening. The ambassador and the students talked until midnight about the Middle East and the difficulties of finding a fair solution to its problems. On other occasions, visitors came to the seminary from Europe, Asia, and South Africa and discussed life in their parts of the world. For Jesse Jackson, these visits were the start of a lifelong concern with international affairs.

The first trips Jackson made overseas were to Africa. In 1971 he went to Lagos, Nigeria, for an Afro-American cultural event. Mrs. Jackson and seven-year-old Santita were with him. The following year he visited Monrovia, Liberia. Back home, he urged black Americans to buy products made in Africa.

In Liberia he had hoped to set up a plan giving dual citizenship to Americans who owned property there. That is, they would become citizens of Liberia without giving up their U.S. citizenship. Despite his efforts, the plan never worked out.

In 1973, there was a crisis in six West African countries. For five years there had been little rain, and farms were producing less and less food. As a result, ten million people were starving in Mauritania, Senegal, Mali, Upper Volta, Niger, and Chad. Jackson called on Americans to help. White and black people from all over the United States responded. In addition to cash donations, sixty-five tons of food and medical supplies were shipped to Africa.

Six years later, Jackson made another trip to Africa. At the invitation of the Congregational churches, he traveled all over South Africa. His former professor, Dr. Howard Schomer, president of Chicago Theological Seminary, went along as his adviser. Jackson spoke to black audiences and white, rich and poor, leaders and followers. Everywhere he went, he was greeted with great excitement. And everywhere he went, he spoke out against apartheid.

Apartheid is a word in Afrikaans (the official language of South Africa) meaning "apartness." It is South Africa's system of government that calls for separate development of the races. There are five times as many black people in South Africa as whites, yet the laws of the country had kept them segregated. The white government decreed where people might live and work and how they could be educated.

Most blacks in South Africa were forced to live far from where they work. Families were often broken up, the parents living and working in different cities. Other people traveled for hours, going to and from low-paying jobs. In spite of all the food South Africa grows, many poor blacks suffered from hunger. Over the years, blacks had been powerless to change things, since they were not allowed to vote.

For about fifty years, black South Africans protested their poor treatment nonviolently. Many were jailed by the government or forced into exile or murdered. In recent years, black protest has become violent and has been reported in headlines around the world.

Apartheid was not discussed publicly in 1979 when the Reverend Jesse Jackson was visiting South Africa. Yet, he stated his harsh judgment of the apartheid system on South Africa's government-owned radio and television. Many businesspeople and antiapartheid leaders in the white community met with him to discuss their country's problems.

His first speech was at the Crossroads squatters camp, on the far edge of the city of Capetown. In spite of a heavy autumn rain and mud, thousands of black people living there came out to hear him. Above the platform where he stood, a banner stretched out, reading, "Welcome, Reverend Jesse Jackson, distinguished son of Mother Africa."

Jackson urged the people to take pride in their blackness. He led them in the same chant he used in the United States: "I am somebody; I may be poor, but I am black, beautiful, and proud."

Some black students at Crossroads had demonstrated for better educational opportunities. He encouraged them to continue their protests and to develop their minds.

Jackson spoke to the people through an interpreter. When the speech was over, the crowd burst into song—hundreds of voices, without a page of music or words to guide them.

At Soweto, a black township near Johannesburg, South

Africa, Jackson wore a zebra-skin cloak and a Basuto straw hat (a loosely woven hat with a curved brim, made by the Basuto people of South Africa). He wore native African clothes as a symbol of his feelings for the people. The audience of ten thousand cheered as he told them that apartheid was evil and, in itself, violent.

By 1984, apartheid had become a major crisis in South Africa. The people and the government had grown more and more violent. Jesse Jackson became a leading spokesperson against apartheid. All across the United States he urged Americans to give up business dealings with South Africa. If the government hurt financially, he was sure it would change its racist attitudes.

He led rallies in front of the South African consular offices in Chicago and New York and at the South African embassy in Washington, D.C. He also flew to England and West Germany to take part in demonstrations there. Protesters carried signs and chanted, "Down with apartheid, free South Africa." During one march in Washington, D.C., the crowd carried fifty coffins—symbols of South Africans recently killed.

As late as January 1986, Jesse Jackson was trying to get a visa to return to South Africa. Although he was turned down, he planned to reapply. He wanted blacks in South Africa to know that many Americans supported them.

In 1979, the same year he visited South Africa and spoke out against apartheid, Jackson made another trip halfway around the world. Because of his many trips by jet airplane, the press nicknamed him Jesse Jetstream. This journey was to the Middle East, where he visited Israel, Lebanon, Syria, Jordan, and Egypt. Jackson wanted to help bring peace to the state of Israel and to its neighbor, Lebanon.

There was a long history of bad relations between Israel and the surrounding Arab countries. The Israelis lived with constant war, bombings, and acts of terrorism. They feared they would be totally destroyed by the army of the PLO (Palestine Liberation Organization). At that time Israeli soldiers were getting back at the Palestinians by bombing southern Lebanon. Jackson hoped to convince both sides to settle things peacefully.

His visit began in Israel. He spoke with the mayor of Jerusalem and toured the Old City of Jerusalem. At the ancient Western Wall, he put on a paper skullcap and prayed silently. At the Holocaust Museum, he viewed photographs of Jews who were abused and killed by the Nazis during World War II. The photographs reminded him of the suffering of black people.

Jackson's next stop was Beirut, Lebanon, where he met with the leader of the PLO, Yasir Arafat. The following day he flew to Cairo to talk with Egypt's president, Anwar el-Sadat. President Sadat already had established good relations with Israel. He told Jackson that any help in settling the Palestinian problem would be welcome.

The next morning Sadat asked Jackson to take a message back to Arafat—to tell him it was the moment for a cease-fire. He sent Jackson back to Beirut in his own jet. Yasir Arafat, however, chose not to follow his advice.

Sadat also asked Jackson to take the same message to Syria's president, Hafez al-Assad. Jackson flew to Damascus with the message, but Assad also turned it down.

No sooner did Jackson return to Beirut than he became sick with a stomach ailment and was taken to the hospital.

That evening Yasir Arafat was at Jackson's bedside. He was friendly, but he made it clear that there would be no cease-fire. Later, the PLO announced that it had ceased all border operations, but there was no mention of stopping action in Israel itself. The problems in the Middle East continued.

In 1983, Jesse Jackson flew to Europe. Most of the trip was taken up with visits to military bases in Great Britain, West Germany, Italy, and Belgium. His main purpose was to carry out a voter registration campaign for American service members, particularly blacks. With an election coming up the next year, he reminded audiences of how important their votes were.

The liveliest part of the trip took place in West Germany. At the base there, Jackson and his aides were allowed to drive tanks and to ride in the most modern helicopters. They watched military shows, where soldiers in tanks staged shooting matches with smoke screens hiding them.

There was another trip to Europe. In 1985, the Reverend Jesse Jackson was invited to speak before the European Parliament in Strasbourg, France. The families of many American service members stationed in Europe came to hear him. It was the fortieth anniversary of the end of World War II, and he spoke about the role of black soldiers in that war. Black soldiers were often given the most dangerous jobs. Many were in the front lines, crawling ahead of the other troops, through land that was dotted with booby traps. Jackson told the audience that his stepfather had been in that war. He fought in Europe for freedom, yet when he returned home, he did not have freedom for himself. It was a few years after the end of World War II that the civil rights movement began in America.

The focus of Jesse Jackson's work has shifted over the years. His earliest work, for Operation Breadbasket and the SCLC, dealt with basic civil rights. Later, economic opportunity became the theme, and resulted in such confrontations as this one, at the national headquarters of A&P in New York.

(Above) As director of Operation PUSH, Jesse Jackson made weekly Saturday morning radio broadcasts from PUSH's auditorium on Chicago's South Side.

(Top right) In the late 1970s Jackson became concerned about students' drug use, drinking, and dropping out from school, so he began Project EXCEL to combat this. Here, at Chicago's Marshall High School, he takes pledges from students joining EXCEL to study hard and avoid drugs and alcohol.

(Bottom right) Although the basic fight for civil rights was considered over in the early 1970s, leaders like Jackson felt that some hard-earned rights were threatened in the 1980s. Here he is marching in 1981 to encourage Congress to extend the Voting Rights Act of 1965.

(Above) When Jackson decided to run for the Democratic Party's nomination for president, he formed a group of supporters called the Rainbow Coalition. This coalition included women and minorities, the people Jackson called the "left-outs" of U.S. society. Here he is pictured with supporters in the "Little Tokyo" section of Los Angeles.

(Opposite page) Jesse Jackson has become increasingly involved in international politics. Besides trips to Africa and Europe, he has visited the Middle East to help get stalled Arab-Israeli peace talks moving. He demonstrated his concern for refugees by visiting a Palestinian camp in Syria *(top left)*. The personal contacts he made during such trips proved valuable later on; when an American serviceman, U.S. Navy Lt. Robert O. Goodman, Jr., was a prisoner in Syria, Jackson was able to convince Syrian president Hafez al-Assad to let Goodman go. Later, President Ronald Reagan praised Jackson's effort when Jackson and Goodman *(far left, in uniform)* returned to the United States.

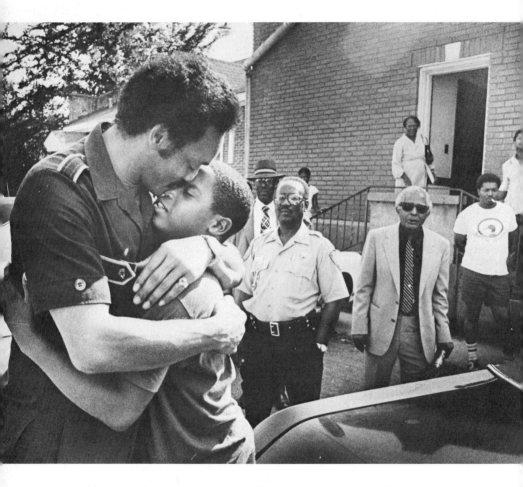

(Above) All the Jackson family was very involved in Jesse's presidential campaign. His son Yusef helped on a voter registration drive in the South.

(Top right) Jesse Jackson addressed this group of striking union shipbuilders during the campaign. In campaigning, Jackson often discussed the conditions faced by America's workers, the farm crisis, and the spending priorities set by the administration of President Ronald Reagan.

(Bottom right) Jesse Jackson shares a laugh with his aide on the campaign trail.

One of the most moving highlights of the 1984 Democratic National Convention was Jesse Jackson's address to the convention.

Chapter/Nine

"Run, Jesse, run!"

In the summer of 1983, Jesse Jackson had a special message for a crowd gathered at the Peachtree Plaza in Atlanta, Georgia. Fifteen hundred PUSH members had come from all over the country to attend a yearly convention. He talked about running for the Democratic Party's nomination for president. In his usual fiery way, Jackson excited the crowd.

He shouted, "Run! Run and you gain self-respect!"

The audience shouted back, "Run! Run! Run!"

He shouted, "If you run, you may lose, but if you don't run, you're guaranteed to lose."

The crowd replied, "Run! Run! Run!"

"Run for the courthouse. Run for the statehouse. Run for the White House. But run!"

The crowd stood up and clapped their hands wildly. They screamed, "Run, Jesse, run!"

Still, Jackson needed to give the idea more thought. He talked to his family and to other black leaders and to the people with whom he worked. He had little money, a small staff, and a late start, but in November of 1983 he made his decision. He would run for president.

Winning the nomination was not the only reason for running. He wanted the country to see that a black person could make a good showing in a presidential race. If he did not win the first time, there would be another chance in four years. He or another black person could try again.

He formed a support group that he named the Rainbow Coalition. The group included people he called "the left-outs"—blacks, poor whites, women, Hispanics, and Arab, Asian, and native Americans. Their slogan became

> Red, yellow, brown, black and white—
> We're all precious in God's sight.

There were seven other Democratic presidential candidates. Most of them had large contributions of money to spend on advertising and traveling. Jackson knew that television commercials and newspaper ads would be too expensive for the Rainbow Coalition. Nor would it have enough money for hotel expenses as Jackson and the staff campaigned around the country. Jackson was sure the other candidates would be much more in the public eye.

But a sudden trip to Syria plunged him into an unexpected whirl of publicity. The eyes of the country were upon him as he flew from Chicago to Damascus to Washington. The reason for all the publicity was a rescue mission he undertook in the Middle East.

Early in December of 1983, a U.S. Navy plane was shot down in Lebanon. It happened during an American raid on Syrian anti-aircraft guns in Lebanon. The Americans were getting back at the Syrians for their attacks on U.S. flights. During the raid, the plane's pilot was killed and the navigator-bombardier was captured by the Syrians.

The captured airman was Lt. Robert O. Goodman, Jr. He had blacked out after being ejected from his plane and, on awakening, found himself locked in a basement cell. His jailers had removed his U.S. Navy clothes, except for his underwear and a T-shirt. He had expected to remain a prisoner a long time.

When it seemed that American officials were making no progress in gaining Lieutenant Goodman's release, it occurred to Jesse Jackson that he might be helpful. He had met Syria's president, Hafez al-Assad, during his trip to the Middle East in 1979. On the strength of that visit, perhaps President Assad would be willing to see him.

In Damascus, Jackson met first with Syria's foreign minister, Abdel Halim Khaddam. They spoke for two hours, but the minister remained firm about keeping the prisoner. The following day, Jackson was granted an interview with President Assad.

The Syrian president did not offer much hope. He reminded Jackson that Lieutenant Goodman had come not as a tourist, but as a soldier, and had been shot down. He said it would upset the Syrian army if he released him.

Jackson first pleaded with Assad on a personal basis to return Lieutenant Goodman to his family. Then he pointed out that by releasing Goodman, Assad would be showing the United States he wanted better relations. If this act led to peace, it would be the right thing to do. He said, "By releasing this soldier, you have nothing to lose and everything to gain."

President Assad promised to reconsider the matter. The next day his foreign minister announced that President Assad was releasing the prisoner. Later the same day, with Lieutenant Goodman at his side, Jackson set out for home.

When he first decided to seek Goodman's release, public opinion at home was mixed. Some people said it was a publicity trick. Others said it might make things worse for the young prisoner. Still others said it was not legal for a private citizen to deal with a foreign government. But Jackson said, "Whoever has the courage to act, should act."

When he returned home, Jackson was greeted as a hero. President Ronald Reagan invited him to the White House and praised him for his success. Jackson was happy to show that problems with other countries could be solved through personal contact.

After that, reporters and photographers followed Jesse Jackson closely as he crossed the country. There was plenty of publicity for his campaign, but money was still a problem.

When the collection plate was passed at rallies, people were asked to give "Jacksons for Jackson"—to give twenty-dollar bills with pictures of President Andrew Jackson. On good nights, several thousand dollars were collected, but still there was not enough money to pay for hotel bills as he and the staff flew from city to city. To keep expenses low, Jackson stayed in the homes of his supporters whenever possible.

In one small town near Pittsburgh, Pennsylvania, an unemployed, white steelworker invited Mr. and Mrs. Jackson to spend the night with his family. Arriving after midnight, they were accompanied by police cars and Secret Service bodyguards in limousines. The quiet street was lit up by the flashing lights of the cars. That night, the Jacksons slept on their host's water bed, while the steelworker and his wife slept on couches in the living room.

The next morning Jackson visited a bread line for unemployed steelworkers and gave them a rousing speech. He said, "Corporations must do a better job of keeping their workers at work. We must have massive training programs for our youth. We must put America back to work."

As he campaigned, more and more people were drawn to him. In Philadelphia, a young black factory worker was riding the bus home when he noticed a large crowd in front of a church. When he heard that the Reverend Jesse Jackson was expected, he got off the bus to wait. He and the crowd waited patiently for several hours. When Jackson finally arrived, he gave an exciting speech. The young factory worker said, "Man, I've been waiting all my life to hear somebody talk like that."

Jackson carried his campaign to people active in peace movements. At a college rally in Madison, Wisconsin, he criticized the defense budget proposed by the other candidates. If elected president, he promised to reduce the defense budget by 20 percent. He was against building an overly large defense system. He said, "You can't hold a missile in one hand and a peace dove in the other."

He also raised the peace issue in the East. One foggy night he had the pilot of his campaign plane make a risky landing in Providence, Rhode Island. The bad weather delayed his arrival, but the black and white supporters in the Baptist church there waited for him.

He shared the platform that night with a popular anti-war figure, Frances Crowe, a sixty-four-year-old woman just released from prison. She had been arrested for painting the words Thou Shalt Not Kill on missile casings in Quonset Point, Rhode Island. Jackson was eager to show his support of Mrs. Crowe. The audience cheered them.

In the South, Jackson combined his campaign talks with a plea to register to vote. The summer before, he had toured the southern states and urged people to register. As a result, 150,000 black people registered for the first time. As he campaigned in 1984, he hoped that thousands more would register and vote for him. Each day he addressed huge crowds as he moved through Florida, Alabama, Georgia, and other southern states.

At university rallies in the North, as well as in the South, Jackson discovered students who had recently become old enough to vote. At his urging, hundreds of young people, black and white, came forward to register.

Another issue that Jackson spoke about was affirmative action. Affirmative action requires that any company or institution receiving federal money must hire a certain number of minority-group members and women. The first affirmative action rule was put in place by President John F. Kennedy and made stronger later by President Lyndon B. Johnson. When President Ronald Reagan came into office, he tried to change that rule.

Jackson campaigned against changing the affirmative action rule. He warned that such a change would take away many of the gains made by blacks during the civil rights struggle. He feared that equal job opportunities for members of minority groups and for women would vanish.

Throughout the campaign, Jackson's family worked hard for him. Jacqueline Jackson gave eloquent speeches on her husband's behalf. Sometimes she spoke in churches, other times on street corners. While she campaigned, volunteer housekeepers cared for her young children at home. (By this time, there were five young Jacksons. Yusef Dubois and Jacqueline II had been born in Chicago.)

For years Mrs. Jackson had spoken out for minority groups, including black women. She had supported the Equal Rights Amendment, and one of her biggest concerns was the rights of all women. She urged women to vote for her husband, because he would work to give them equal opportunities.

The four older Jackson children were also keen campaigners. Speaking on their father's behalf was not new to Santita, Jesse, Junior, and Jonathan Luther. For several years they had picketed, demonstrated, boycotted, and spoken to youth groups. For thirteen-year-old Yusef, it was a new experience.

At that time, Santita (Sandy), age twenty-one, was a student at Howard University in Washington, D.C. Her friends were accustomed to her father's secretary suddenly appearing in the library to whisk Sandy away for a campaign talk. To avoid missing classes, she rarely went farther than nearby Maryland and Virginia. She knew the issues and believed in them as deeply as her father did.

The two older boys were high school seniors. Jesse, Junior, nineteen, attended St. Albans High School in Washington, D.C., and Jonathan, eighteen, went to Whitney Young High School in Chicago. Yusef also studied in Chicago.

The boys campaigned only on weekends. They never seemed to tire of shaking hands with people in the crowd and signing autographs. They also studied the issues carefully and came well prepared to speak.

All three boys campaigned in Indiana, as well as in Arkansas, Mississippi, and Kentucky. During the Indiana tour, Jesse, Junior, told his audiences, "This campaign is not fighting for social service, we're fighting for social change." He spoke of the need to change the condition of the poor. Jonathan told young people it was time to act. He said, "Let us not look back twenty years from now and see how we sat idly by and did nothing."

Jonathan had often said he would like to pattern himself after his father. "It is important to carry on the dreams of black people," he said.

Yusef, Jonathan, and Jesse, Junior, traveled with their father to Central America and Cuba during the campaign. It was not exactly a private family journey. With them were sixty-three reporters and photographers and twenty-seven Secret Service agents. There were also about twenty aides, including Jackson's press secretary, a Latin American advisor, a speech writer, a translator, and several ministers.

Jesse Jackson went to Latin America to show his interest in peace. He feared the wars going on in Central America could spread to the United States.

Their first stop was Panama City, where Jackson met with Panama's president, Jorge Illuera, and foreign minister, Oyden Ortega. He spent most of the next day with four exiled leaders of El Salvador's rebel forces. They asked Jackson to take a message to El Salvador's president. They wanted the president to know they were willing to return to their country to discuss a cease-fire of the war going on there.

Flying to El Salvador the next day, Jackson delivered the message to President José Napoleon Duarte. They met at the Presidential Palace in San Salvador. President Duarte promised to take the proposal to the people of El Salvador.

Jackson's next stop was Cuba. He was greeted at the airport in Havana by President Fidel Castro. The two men climbed into a Russian-made limousine and led a parade of automobiles to the city.

The next day Jackson was to visit the jail in Havana. Prison authorities told the inmates to start a baseball game before his arrival. (A reporter learned that the prisoners called baseball the "visitors' game" because they were allowed to play only when guests came.) Jackson arrived quite late, and the prisoners continued to play while waiting for him. They ended up playing seventy innings.

Later there were serious talks, and Jackson persuaded President Castro to free forty-eight prisoners. Twenty-two were Americans, most held on minor drug charges. Twenty-six were political prisoners—some Cuban, some American.

Jackson spent the next day in Nicaragua, calling for an end to that country's war. Then he returned to Cuba to fly back to the United States with the freed prisoners.

The campaign ended in July 1984, at the convention of the Democratic Party in San Francisco. Walter Mondale, a former vice-president, won the party's nomination. Jesse Jackson was pleased with the way the campaign had gone. He had forced the other candidates to think about issues important to black people. And he had given black youngsters the hope that some day even they could grow up to be president.

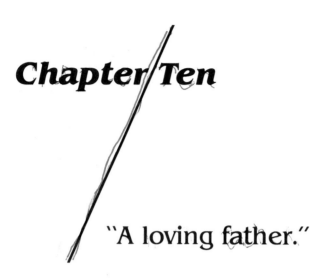

Chapter Ten

"A loving father."

After his 1984 campaign, Jesse Jackson divided his time between his Rainbow Coalition office in Washington, D.C., and trips to other cities. On weekends he flew home to be with his family.

He and his wife Jacqueline live in a large, comfortable house on Chicago's South Side. Their youngest daughter, Jacqueline II (Jacky), is the only child living at home in 1986. She goes to a private school in Chicago. When Jacky gets lonesome, she picks up the phone and makes a long-distance call to her sister or brothers. The Jacksons' monthly telephone bills are usually very large.

Sandy and Yusef are students in Washington, D.C. Sandy is a premedical senior at Howard University, while Yusef goes to St. Albans High School. Jesse, Junior, and Jonathan Luther (Jonnie), attend their father's old school, A&T (now North Carolina Agricultural and Technical State University), in Greensboro. Jesse, Junior, is thinking about studying law, while Jonathan is considering business.

The Jacksons plan to move into a second home in Washington, D.C. It will be closer to Jackson's Rainbow Coalition office and more convenient for the older children. The new house is really an old house—one hundred years old. Jackson calls it "a raggedy house," and says the family will have fun fixing it up before they move in.

Still another house is theirs. Not long ago, Jackson bought the home where his parents used to live, in Greenville, South Carolina. That city is where he now votes in elections.

The Jackson home in Chicago is a lively place, especially when all the children are there. A basketball hoop in the backyard is a favorite meeting place for the family. The men play a fast game, while the women sit on the lawn and keep score.

Working out on the basketball court is a good way for Jesse Jackson to relax. When he is at home (and if the weather permits) a few of the ministers from PUSH may join him at five or six o'clock in the morning. After three or four games, they change their clothes and go to work. During the summer months, they also play in the evening, beginning about seven o'clock and finishing at sundown. Between games and afterwards, they discuss work problems.

When the children were small, they stood around with kids from the neighborhood, watching the men play. Every chance they had, the kids ran around the court and tried to shoot the ball into the basket. The adults had to shoo them away.

As the Jackson boys grew up, they joined the adult games. Soon they were playing better than their seniors. There were private games, too, when father and sons talked about personal things. They still go on. Mrs. Jackson says, "On the basketball court the boys are always wrestling with new thoughts and new ideas, raising questions with their daddy."

Sandy and her sister Jacky find other times to talk with their dad. They discuss anything and everything with him. Sandy says, "In addition to loving my father, I like him very much. He is a very open, warm person."

Once the older children were away at school, holidays became the only times the family could get together. When everyone comes home, Mrs. Jackson takes a break from her work. During the year she lectures to groups in Chicago and other cities. At times she travels to other countries on fact-finding trips, and gives her husband firsthand reports. But she is almost always at home when her family is there.

For the Jacksons, Christmas is the most important holiday of the year. The whole month of December is set aside for a continuous birthday party for Christ. No gifts are given, but each day is a celebration. Mrs. Jackson decorates about a dozen Christmas trees with lights and tinsel and sets them up in different rooms of their big house. The decorations are not complete until wreaths are hung on many of the windows.

Then the cooking begins. Sandy and Jacky and their brothers all lend a hand. The friends they bring home for the holidays also find their way to the kitchen to help with the cooking, as well as the eating. Delicious-smelling pies, puddings, and cakes emerge from the oven in a steady stream. Mrs. Jackson believes that nothing can take the place of good food, lovingly prepared.

Love enters into everything the family does. In Mrs.

Jackson's words, her husband is "a loving father—one of the most loving fathers in the world." When he comes home, he hugs and kisses each person—his sons, as well as his daughters and his wife. Being able to love all his children freely goes back to Jesse Jackson's memories of his natural father. He, too, was quick to embrace and kiss Jesse and his other sons, with no embarrassment.

Jesse Jackson still remembers the pain he felt at being separated from his natural father when he was young. As a result, he spends as much time as possible with his own children. Being away from home so much presents a problem. One solution has been to take his children along when he travels. (His two older sons were with him when he rescued the Navy airman in Syria, and later, during a visit to the Pope in Rome.) During the summer months, they generally take turns going with him. Their interest in his work has given them a broad education.

That special education started early. While the Jackson children were growing up, family outings were not the usual kind. Instead of going to museums or movies or places of entertainment, their parents took them along to rallies and meetings. Early in life they heard important ideas discussed and learned about community problems.

Today, when the Reverend Jesse Jackson cannot keep a speaking appointment, one of the older children may speak in his place. They keep up with current issues. If they have been at school and missed some of his talks, they call his press secretary to ask for copies. They share many of their father's dreams.

Two sons also shared a jail cell with him one night in Washington, D.C. In the spring of 1985, Jesse, Junior, and

Jonathan Luther marched with their father in an anti-apartheid protest outside the South African Embassy. As father and sons crossed their arms and linked hands, the police arrested them.

In jail with them that night were twenty-five young boys, some arrested on charges of drugs or murder. All the boys were between the ages of twelve and sixteen, and not one had a father at home. The Jacksons were saddened by their stories. Later Jesse Jackson said, "To talk with those boys about how they got in jail, with my sons there, was an important experience for all of us."

Jacqueline Jackson is still amazed by her husband's patience and his ability to love everyone. In her eyes, he is bigger than others because of what she says is "his capacity to understand justice and love." He makes time in his busy schedule to see people who need to talk to him. Yet, she says, "he works, teaches, holds on to his ideas and never gives up."

In private life, Jesse Jackson is different than he appears in public. Gone are the booming voice and forceful personality. He is quiet and thoughtful, letting others do the talking. When he speaks, his voice is soft and low. Although he has a keen sense of humor, he is serious most of the time. He seldom smiles.

At home, he rises early in the morning and begins the day by writing. He may work on a speech or his weekly newspaper column. He works quietly, with the sound of music in the background.

During the week, his days are filled with traveling, speeches, meetings, and workshops. At night he gets little sleep, but he catches up on rest during the day with catnaps on planes and in taxis.

His drive to get things done sometimes causes him to neglect his health. Because of the sickle-cell trait, he is quick to come down with illnesses, though he always looks healthy. The only outward sign of the blood disease is the sweat that runs down his face, noticeable when he speaks in public. When he suspects he is becoming ill, he gets extra sleep and eats more carefully.

Apart from Mrs. Jackson, probably no one knows the Reverend Jesse Jackson as well as his press secretary, the Reverend Frank Watkins. For seventeen years they have worked and traveled together, played basketball together, and campaigned together. Watkins calls Jackson the most courageous man he has ever known. It is not his courage to risk being arrested that Watkins talks about. It is the courage to risk a new idea, when there is no way of being certain that the idea will work.

Early in his career, Jackson had the courage to risk boycotts against large, successful companies. Later he risked forming the Black Expo to help black businesses. Then he risked setting up his own organization, PUSH, followed by PUSH Expo and PUSH for Excellence. Over the years he has organized hundreds of boycotts and marches. His run for the presidential nomination may have been the largest risk of all. The courage to take such risks is what Frank Watkins calls Jackson's biggest strength.

Another strength is his way of making complicated ideas seem simple. Whenever he deals with a confusing idea, he breaks it down into simple words before presenting it to an audience. It is something he learned to do a long time ago. When he was studying to be a minister, one of his professors noticed the way he helped small children understand

complicated religious ideas. Today Jackson tells his staff to
think about how they would describe an idea to their own
families, before talking to a group.

When Jesse Jackson joined the race for the presidential
nomination, he resigned as director of Operation PUSH.
Presiding over seventy-five chapters and more than fifty
thousand members was too much for an active political
candidate. He turned over the leadership to a woman, the
Reverend Willie Barrow.

As founder of PUSH, Jackson is still a very active
member and takes part in all major decision making. And
no matter where he travels during the week, he returns to
Chicago for the Saturday rallies.

By eight o'clock on Saturday mornings, dozens of people are waiting to consult him at Operation PUSH headquarters. They come from all over the city, and even farther
away. They join him for breakfast, and he has advice and
encouragement for everyone.

By ten o'clock he is on the stage of the PUSH church,
ready for the weekly broadcast. As he speaks to the hundreds of people gathered in the auditorium in front of him,
a microphone carries his words to the radio audience.
Mostly black, the audience in the church often includes
young students, famous athletes, politicans, and Hollywood
friends of Jackson.

Most of the time, he delivers his sermon in a business suit
and a tie. On warm days he appears in shirt sleeves. A
white-robed choir and a swinging gospel band share the
morning's program. The audience sways and claps its hands
in time to the music. When Jackson begins to speak, his
voice is low and the auditorium is quiet. The background

music is soft. His sermon is partly political, partly religious. As he raises his voice, the band and the choir increase their volume. Soon he is shouting, but his words are nearly drowned by the rising sounds of the singing voices, the guitars, the drums, and the clapping hands. When the sermon is over, the audience applauds wildly and people rush over to shake his hand. The glow on his face surely must mean that now he is somebody, just as Aunt Tibby had asked.

* * * * *

As he has done all his adult life, the Reverend Jesse Jackson continues to work for human rights, social justice, and peace. He was pursuing these goals in 1985 when he visited Pope John Paul II in Rome. They talked about apartheid in South Africa, famine in Africa, and world peace. In Geneva, later that year, he met with Mikhail Gorbachev, head of the Russian government. They discussed nuclear tests, the problems in South Africa, and the plight of Jews in Russia who were not allowed to leave the country. He also lent his support to farmers who were in danger of losing their farms in the United States.

Human rights, social justice, and peace are also the goals of the Rainbow Coalition, the organization Jackson formed when he ran for the presidential nomination. He is working to build the coalition into a permanent political organization. In his own words, the Reverend Jesse Jackson says

I will remain active in the forefront of our quest for freedom and human dignity, so long as I live and am able of mind and body.

Postscript

"Our time has come."

On July 17, 1984, the Reverend Jesse Jackson delivered a speech to the Democratic National Convention in San Francisco, California. It has been called one of the great speeches of modern American history. Following are some excerpts from that talk.

This is not a perfect party. We are not a perfect people. Yet, we are called to a perfect mission: our mission, to feed the hungry, to clothe the naked, to house the homeless, to teach the illiterate, to provide jobs for the jobless, and to choose the human race over the nuclear race.

This campaign has taught me much: that leaders must be tough enough to fight, tender enough to cry, human enough to make mistakes, humble enough to admit them, strong enough to absorb the pain, and resilient enough to bounce back and keep on moving. For leaders, the pain is often intense. But you must smile through your tears and keep moving with the faith that there is a brighter side somewhere.

Our flag is red, white, and blue, but our nation is rainbow—red, yellow, brown, black, and white—we're all precious in God's sight. America is not like a blanket—one piece of unbroken cloth, the same color, the same texture, the same size. America is more like a quilt—many patches, many pieces, many colors, many sizes, all woven and held together by a common thread.

Young America, dream. Choose the human race over the nuclear race. Bury the weapons and don't burn the people. Dream of a new value system. Teachers, who teach for life, and not just for a living, teach because they can't help it. Dream of lawyers more concerned with justice than a judgeship. Dream of doctors more concerned with public health than personal wealth. Dream of preachers and priests who will prophesy and not just profiteer. Preach and Dream. Our time has come.

Our time has come. Suffering breeds character. Character breeds faith. And in the end, faith will not disappoint.

Appendix/One

A Brief History of the Civil Rights Movement

In the early 1800s, most blacks in the United States were considered slaves and had no rights as citizens. However, during the Civil War, in 1863, President Abraham Lincoln issued the Emancipation Proclamation, freeing blacks from slavery. After the war, the Civil Rights Act of 1866 guaranteed the rights of all citizens. It allowed blacks to vote, to take part in state government, and to hold public office.

Despite these laws, most blacks did not gain real freedom or equal rights. Many were unable to find jobs or participate in government. In the South, freed blacks often continued to work for their old masters on cotton and tobacco plantations. Many plantation owners threatened to dismiss black workers who tried to vote.

In the late 1800s, many blacks moved to cities and towns to look for work. City jobs were hard to find, and blacks who did find jobs were paid low wages, in part because the unions did not accept black members. Finding adequate housing presented another problem. Groups of white people often rioted against blacks who tried to work and live in their areas.

The federal government did not enforce the early civil rights laws. Gradually, blacks lost their rights to an equal share of American life. By 1907, every state in the South had passed new state and local laws that segregated (separated) blacks from whites in public places.

When they realized that the government offered them little support, black people began to develop their own plans for improving their conditions. By the early 1900s, a number of eloquent black leaders had emerged. They spoke out and formed movements and organizations to help black people achieve full equality in American life.

In the late 1940s and early 1950s, the U.S. Supreme Court issued several rulings designed to create equality in education. Early rulings stated that blacks must receive the same quality of education as whites. Equality could be achieved through separate but equal schools for blacks and whites or through integrated schools (schools attended by both blacks and whites). In 1954, the Court ruled that segregation in public schools was unequal, and white schools were ordered to desegregate (allow blacks to attend).

Many southern communities were slow in desegregating their public schools. For example, in 1957, the governor of Little Rock, Arkansas, Orville E. Faubus, defied a court order to integrate Little Rock Central High School. He used the Arkansas National Guard to keep black students from entering. President Dwight D. Eisenhower forced the governor to comply with the ruling by sending federal troops to escort the black students into the school.

Racial discrimination in housing and recreation was also declared illegal in the 1950s. These decisions inspired blacks to take action against other types of discrimination.

In 1955, Rosa Parks, a black seamstress in Montgomery, Alabama, refused to give up her seat to a white person on a local bus. She was arrested for violating a city law that required segregation of blacks and whites on city buses. Parks's arrest led to a citywide protest by blacks, who refused to ride the city buses. Their boycott lasted 382 days and was guided by Dr. Martin Luther King, Jr. On December 13, 1956, the U.S. Supreme Court ruled that segregation on public buses in Montgomery violated the Constitution.

In 1957, the Southern Christian Leadership Conference was formed, headed by Dr. Martin Luther King, Jr. The SCLC urged blacks to work for integration and full equality through nonviolent means. By 1960, a number of other civil rights groups banded together to end segregation and discrimination.

The Student Nonviolent Coordinating Committee (SNCC) was formed in 1960 by a group of black and white college students. This group worked with the Southern Christian Leadership Conference, the Congress of Racial Equality, and the National Association for the Advancement of Colored People. They protested discrimination against blacks in hotels, restaurants, and other public areas by organizing sit-ins, boycotts, and marches. As a result of their combined efforts, discrimination ended in some public places.

But discrimination continued in many cities and towns. In 1963, black civil rights leaders organized a march against discrimination. The march took place in Washington, D.C., in August of 1963, and it was the largest protest demonstration in U.S. history. About 250,000 blacks and whites gathered to urge Congress to pass civil rights laws that would end discrimination and allow blacks equal access to public areas. Dr. Martin Luther King, Jr., told the crowd about his dream that one day all Americans would enjoy equality and justice.

President John F. Kennedy met with the civil rights leaders at the White House, and promised to push through civil rights laws. However, in November of 1963, President Kennedy was assassinated. The new president, Lyndon B. Johnson, persuaded Congress to pass the laws proposed by Kennedy. The following July, the Civil Rights Act of 1964 was signed. This act outlawed racial discrimination in public places, and called for equal opportunities in employment and education.

Despite these new laws, few blacks were actively involved in federal and state government. Many blacks in the South were still not allowed to vote. In January of 1965, Dr. Martin Luther King, Jr., began a voter registration drive in Selma, Alabama. White opposition was violent. Three people were killed, and hundreds were beaten and arrested during the demonstrations. Dr. King tried to lead marchers from Selma to Montgomery, the capital of Alabama. Twice they were turned back by state troopers. The third time the marchers were protected by federal troops. On March 25, thousands of black and white people marched into Montgomery. Gathering on the steps of the capitol building, Dr. King and others denounced Alabama leaders for denying voting rights to blacks.

The months of protest in Alabama influenced a new

voting rights bill, signed in August of 1965. The bill prohibited the use of a poll tax, which had kept many blacks from voting. In addition, the new bill called for federal agents to register black voters if they were turned away by local officials. Thousands of blacks were able to vote for the first time.

More barriers were lowered when President Johnson pushed through an affirmative action program that gave blacks equal opportunities in business and education. By taking advantage of the new opportunities, many blacks were able to increase their incomes and better their living conditions. As a result, the black middle class grew larger.

By the 1960s, a number of blacks had distinguished themselves in professional sports, in the arts, and in other fields. In spite of this progress, many blacks continued to encounter racism in employment, housing, and law enforcement.

During the 1960s, race riots exploded in ghettos across the country. The violence brought many deaths and injuries, and much destruction of property. To study the cause of the riots, President Johnson established the Kerner Commission. In March of 1968, the commission reported that the problems were largely due to prejudice based on race. Many whites were against blacks without sufficient reason, and this prejudice affected every aspect of blacks' lives. The commission recommended specific programs to improve ghetto life and called for changes in the racial attitudes of whites.

With the assassination of Dr. Martin Luther King, Jr., on April 4, 1968, race riots broke out again in black communities across the United States. Following King's death,

President Johnson persuaded Congress to approve the Civil Rights Act of 1968. Also known as the Fair Housing Act, it forbade racial discrimination in the sale and rental of housing.

At this time, a number of black militant groups decided that the focus of the civil rights movement needed to shift. These groups felt that white attitudes against blacks could not be changed. They urged black Americans to live apart from whites and, in some cases, they advocated violence to preserve their rights. The groups who supported this viewpoint included the Black Muslims, the Black Panthers, and the Black Power Movement.

The Black Panthers organized in 1965, after the riots in the Watts section of the Los Angeles ghetto. At first the group advocated revolution, but later it changed its goals and supported peaceful solutions to employment and education problems. Leaders of the Black Power Movement, organized in 1966, urged blacks to gain political and economic control of their own communities, and to reject white standards.

Blacks have gained much in the course of the civil rights movement. An increased number of black students have enrolled in high schools and colleges since 1970. Many schools have developed black studies programs, emphasizing black heritage. Black musical and theater groups have also become active, and Afro-American museums have been established in many cities. Black-owned businesses have increased sharply in recent years. More blacks are also taking part in every level of government, either by election or by appointment. In almost every field, blacks have won national recognition for outstanding service.

Many of these gains resulted from affirmative action programs. In the 1980s, however, court decisions were unclear and seemed to threaten affirmative action. Some blacks charged President Ronald Reagan's administration with weakening the enforcement of civil rights laws, and with hurting the poor by cutting federal welfare programs. President Reagan denied these charges.

Many black Americans still face economic problems. By the end of 1984, the unemployment rate for blacks was twice as high as for whites. More than one-third of the nation's black families had an income of less than ten thousand dollars, the official poverty line for a family of four.

In the eyes of many black leaders, the solution to black problems lies in politics. They urge blacks to vote and to run for public office. Since 1960, a number of black mayors have been elected in cities across the United States. In 1984, civil rights leader Jesse Jackson made a bid for the Democratic presidential nomination. Though he lost the race, he inspired hope in the hearts of many.

Appendix/Two

Black Leaders
Who Influenced
Jesse Jackson

The Reverend Ralph David Abernathy
(Born March 11, 1926, Linden, Alabama)
Rev. Ralph David Abernathy is a Baptist minister who helped Dr. Martin Luther King, Jr., establish the Southern Christian Leadership Conference. He was one of King's chief aides and worked with King to organize the bus boycott in Montgomery, Alabama, in 1955. After Dr. King's death in April of 1968, Dr. Abernathy assumed national leadership of the SCLC. He was president of the SCLC until 1977, and he headed the Poor People's Campaign in Washington, D.C., in May of 1968. Rev. Abernathy led other demonstrations in the South, calling attention to poverty and protesting job discrimination and segregation.

Frederick Douglass
(Born 1817, near Easton, Maryland; died 1895)
Frederick Douglass was an abolitionist and civil rights leader who helped fugitive slaves escape into Canada, staged

sit-ins on Massachusetts railroads, and led a fight for school integration in Rochester, New York. He was born into slavery, but escaped to New York and freedom when he was twenty-one. Within three years, he became known as an eloquent speaker. In the United States and abroad, he spoke to both white and black audiences about slavery, the rights of women, the rights of all people everywhere, and world peace. He worked to make white people aware of the evils of slavery and to inspire black people in their struggle for freedom and equality. In 1889, Douglass was appointed U.S. minister to Haiti.

William E. B. Du Bois
(Born 1868, Great Barrington, Massachusetts; died 1963)

William E. B. Du Bois was a civil rights leader for fifty years and the first black to receive a Ph.D. from Harvard. He headed the Department of History and Economics at Atlanta University, where he conducted annual conferences on black life in the United States. At each conference, he presented a study describing life in a different black community, in the hope that racial prejudice would lessen if white people knew more about black people. His book *The Souls of Black Folks* was a collection of essays on race and politics, and was read by people around the world.

In 1905, Du Bois helped start the Niagara Movement, a drive that demanded full equality for blacks in American life. In 1909, the Niagara Movement became the National Association for the Advancement of Colored People. Du Bois taught blacks to fight for their rights as human beings and to have pride in their black heritage. He was also interested in Africa, and led a movement to guide Africans in developing political and economic independence. Toward the end of his life, Du Bois moved to Africa, and he died in Ghana.

Paul Laurence Dunbar
(Born 1872, Dayton, Ohio; died 1906)

Paul Laurence Dunbar was the first nationally known black poet. He published his first poems at the age of sixteen, his first book of poetry at the age of twenty-one, and two other volumes at the age of twenty-four. After his books were published, he was offered work as a reader for the Library of Congress. He traveled widely and gave poetry readings at schools, churches, and other institutions. Dunbar's poetry was simple and often humorous. Written in black dialect, his poems gave blacks a sense of pride in their heritage. Read widely by whites, his poetry was the first to make dialect an acceptable literary form. Dunbar also wrote short stories and novels.

Marcus Garvey
(Born 1887, Jamaica; died 1940)

Marcus Garvey was dedicated to improving working conditions for black people. In 1914, he founded the Universal Negro Improvement Association (UNIA) in Jamaica. In 1916, he took the movement to New York's Harlem, where he started a newspaper, *The Negro World*, and a chain of UNIA groceries and laundries. His goals were to promote unity among blacks and pride in their heritage. He was particularly concerned for the welfare of African blacks.

In the 1920s, Garvey organized the Back to Africa

movement, which encouraged American blacks to move to Africa. This movement was supported by between one and four million American blacks. To take black people to Africa, he started a shipping line, the Black Star, which failed because of mismanagement. In 1923, Garvey was sentenced to prison for fraud in raising money for his steamship company. The UNIA collapsed following his arrest.

The Reverend Martin Luther King, Jr.
(Born 1929, Atlanta, Georgia; died 1968)
Rev. Martin Luther King, Jr., was ordained a Baptist minister at the age of eighteen. He earned degrees from Morehouse College and Crozer Theological Seminary, and was awarded a Ph.D. from Harvard. In 1954, he became pastor of the Dexter Avenue Baptist Church in Montgomery, Alabama. In 1955 and 1956, he led the successful black boycott of Montgomery's segregated buses. He was elected the first president of the Southern Christian Leadership Conference in 1957, and became national leader of the civil rights movement.

King was dedicated to ending racial discrimination, poverty, and war. Although he was jailed frequently, he never gave up his policy of passive resistance to oppression. In 1964, Dr. King was awarded the Nobel Peace Prize for bringing peaceful change to America. In April of 1968, he was killed by an assassin in Memphis, Tennessee.

Malcolm X (Malcolm Little)
(Born 1925, Omaha, Nebraska; died 1965)
Malcolm Little was the son of a Baptist minister who supported black nationalist Marcus Garvey. In 1952, while in

prison on charges of burglary, Little converted to the Black Muslims, a militant Islamic group that believed in separation of the races. As a member of this group, he adopted the name of Malcolm X. In 1953, he became assistant minister of a temple in Detroit.

For many years, Malcolm X was a leading spokesperson for the Black Muslims. However, during a trip to Mecca, the holy city of Islam, in Saudi Arabia, Malcolm X discovered that the true Muslim believes in love and brotherhood of the races, not in separation and hate. He resigned from the Black Muslims in 1964 and formed his own group, the Organization of Afro-American Unity (OAAU), which denounced racism and segregation. In 1965, he was assassinated at an OAAU rally in New York City, by three men known to be supporters of the Black Muslims.

The Reverend Leon Sullivan
(Born 1922, Charleston, West Virginia)
Rev. Leon Sullivan was a Baptist minister in Philadelphia in the 1950s. He led quiet boycotts in the black ghettos, advising black consumers not to buy products where they were not allowed to work. Thousands of jobs for blacks became available through his efforts. He then set up a job-training program for blacks, called the Opportunities Industrialization Center. His programs have since spread across the United States and to other countries.

Booker T. Washington
(Born 1856, Virginia; died 1915)
Booker T. Washington was born into slavery. He began his education at the age of sixteen, at Hampton Institute, in

Hampton, Virginia, a school for blacks where general education was combined with trade education. Later he became a teacher at Hampton Institute and started a night school. In 1881, he founded Tuskegee Normal and Industrial Institute at Tuskegee, Alabama. The school trained black teachers in general education as well as in trades such as bricklaying and carpentry. The institute began as a high school, and later offered some college courses. It became the Tuskegee Institute in 1837. Today it offers professional degrees in many fields.

Washington was an eloquent speaker, lecturing in the United States and in Europe on race relations, education, and the importance of vocational training as a means of economic independence for blacks.

Bibliography

Books

Adams, A. John, and Joan Martin Burke. *Civil Rights, A CBS News Reference Book*. New York: Bowker, 1970.

Baker, Patricia. *Martin Luther King*. Hove, East Sussex, England: Wayland, 1974.

Dennis, R. Ethel. *The Black People of America*. New York: McGraw-Hill, 1970.

Drotning, Phillip T., and Wesley South. "The Now Look in Religion." In *Up from the Ghetto*. New York: Cowles, 1970.

Frost, David. "When Whites Are Unemployed . . . " In *The Americans*. Briarcliff Manor, N.Y.: Stein & Day, 1970.

Hornsby, Alton, Jr. *The Black Almanac*. Barron's Educational Series. Woodbury, N.Y.: Barron, 1973.

————. "Black Americans" in *World Book Encyclopedia*, 1986.

"Jesse Louis Jackson." In *Current Biography Yearbook*, 196-99. New York: H. W. Wilson, 1970.

Hughes, Langston, Milton Meltzer, and C. Eric Lincoln. *A Pictorial History of Black Americans*. 4th ed. New York: Crown, 1973.

Landess, Thomas, and Richard Quinn. *Jesse Jackson and the Politics of Race.* Ottawa, Ill.: Jameson Books, 1985.

Reynolds, Barbara A. *Jesse Jackson: America's David.* Formerly published as *Jesse Jackson: The Man, The Movement, The Myth.* Washington, D.C.: JFJ Associates, 1985.

Stone, Eddie. *Jesse Jackson.* Los Angeles: Holloway House, 1979.

Travis, Dempsey J. *An Autobiography of Black Chicago.* Chicago: Urban Research Institute, 1981.

Westman, Paul. *Jesse Jackson, I Am Somebody.* Minneapolis: Dillon Press, 1981.

Articles

Barnes, Fred. "The Jackson Tour." *New Republic* (July 30, 1984): 18-21.

"Black Pocketbook Power." *Time* (March 1, 1968): 17.

Cheers, D. Michael. "Campaigning for Jackson Is a Family Affair." *Jet* (April 2, 1984): 6-8.

―――. "Lt. Robert Goodman: The Story Behind His Rescue." *Ebony* (March 1984): 155-62.

―――. "Shocking Plight of Black Life in Tunica, Mississippi." *Jet* (August 12, 1985): 26-31.

Danaher, Kevin. "South Africa: Hunger in a Land of Plenty." *Food First Action Alert.* A fact sheet published by Food First Books, San Francisco (1985).

"Further Travels with Jesse." *Time* (October 15, 1979): 63.

Goldman, P. " 'Run, Jesse, Run': A Crusade Is Launched." *Newsweek* (November-December 1984): 49-52.

"Interview with the Rev. Jesse Jackson." *Ebony* (June 1981): 155ff.

Jackson, Jesse Louis. "The Rainbow Coalition." Address to the Democratic National Convention, July 17, 1984. *Vital Speeches of the Day* (November 15, 1984): 77-81.

"Jesse Jackson: One Leader Among Many." *Time* (April 6, 1970): 13ff.

Klein, Joe. "Travels with Jesse." *People Weekly* (April 23, 1984): 32-37.

Levine, Richard. "Jesse Jackson: Heir to Dr. King?" *Harper's* (March 1969): 58-70.

Massaquoi, Hans J. "Mrs. Jacqueline L. Jackson: 'I'd Make a Great First Lady.' " *Ebony* (July 1984): 25ff.

Merriner, Jim. "The '84 Race Is Over, But Jackson's Still Running." *Chicago Sun Times* (October 13, 1985): 14ff.

Morganthau, Tom, and Sylvester Monroe. "Jesse's European Jet Stream." *Newsweek* (September 26, 1983): 34.

Page, Clarence. " 'I Am Somebody!' . . . But Who?" *Washington Monthly* (February 1980): 26-36.

Pekkanen, John. "Black Hope, White Hope." *Life* (November 21, 1969): 67ff.

Saar, John, and Peter Younghusband. "Jesse Jackson Takes On Pretoria." *Newsweek* (August 13, 1979): 36.

Serrin, William. "Jesse Jackson: 'I Am . . .' (Somebody)." *New York Times Magazine* (July 9, 1972): 14ff.

Smothers, Ronald. "The Impact of Jesse Jackson." *New York Times Magazine* (March 4, 1984): 40ff.

Strausberg, Chinta. "Vets to Tell 'Untold Story.' " *Chicago Defender* (May 28, 1985): 3.

Index